TURNING
FIERCE DOGS
FRIENDLY

KELLIE SNIDER, MS

Turning Fierce Dogs Friendly

CompanionHouse Books™ is an imprint of Fox Chapel Publishers International Ltd.

Project Team
Vice President–Content: Christopher Reggio
Editor: Amy Deputato
Copy Editor: Laura Taylor
Design: Mary Ann Kahn
Index: Elizabeth Walker

ISBN 978-1-62187-175-0

The Cataloging-in-Publication Data is on file with the Library of Congress.

This book has been published with the intent to provide accurate and authoritative information in regard to the subject matter within. While every precaution has been taken in the preparation of this book, the author and publisher expressly disclaim any responsibility for any errors, omissions, or adverse effects arising from the use or application of the information contained herein. The techniques and suggestions are used at the reader's discretion and are not to be considered a substitute for veterinary care. If you suspect a medical problem, consult your veterinarian.

Fox Chapel Publishing
903 Square Street
Mount Joy, PA 17552

Fox Chapel Publishers International Ltd.
7 Danefield Road, Selsey (Chichester)
West Sussex PO20 9DA, U.K.

www.facebook.com/companionhousebooks

We are always looking for talented authors. To submit an idea, please send a brief inquiry to acquisitions@foxchapelpublishing.com.

Printed and bound in Singapore
20 19 18 17   2 4 6 8 10 9 7 5 3 1

CONTENTS

INTRODUCTION

This book is about teaching an animal to perform safe, friendly behaviors instead of aggressive and dangerous, or fearful and debilitating, behaviors. Dr. Israel Goldiamond coined the term *constructional approach* in the 1970s to describe a method of building (or constructing) new behaviors for human learners—behaviors that work better than what they are currently doing—that enable them to interact with their environments in socially acceptable ways. The Constructional Aggression Treatment (or CAT, as it has come to be known) for dogs is a process that Dr. Jesús Rosales-Ruiz directed and I, as his graduate research assistant, performed as part of a series of research on building appropriate behaviors in aggressive dogs. It was a brilliant, though sometimes frightening, learning opportunity for me, for which I am eternally grateful.

We conducted CAT with aggressive dogs, but it's important to note that the constructional approach can address behavior problems other than aggression and that it works with species other than dogs. Dr. Rosales and his graduate students have worked with goats, sheep, a hamster, cats, llamas, a sparrow, dogs, a cow, horses, and humans. CAT has also been used by other trainers with a fruit bat (this large bat liked to sneak up behind his keepers and whack them on the back of their heads with his foot), various species of parrot, an iguana, pigeons, anoles (color-changing lizards common in the southern United States), green frogs, red crowned cranes, a person who was afraid of rats, rats who were afraid of people, a crow, rabbits, a chimpanzee, a giraffe, a common eland, fennec foxes, a jaguar, a baboon, blue-eyed lemurs, griffon vultures, skunks, a peregrine falcon, pot-bellied pigs, a javelina, an eagle, and a hare. And these are just the ones I know about. I listed all these species so it won't seem quite as strange when I tell you how I got involved in working with aggressive dogs.

I went back to school in the middle of my life after many years of starting and stopping my education. I started five different university majors that didn't hold my interest or that held my interest but weren't practical. One thing that did hold my interest was animals, but I didn't want to be a vet, and that is pretty much where my mind went when I thought about working with them.

In the mid-1990s, my family got a big pink parrot, a Moluccan cockatoo named Coral. She was officially my bird, but she loved my husband and took to biting me like a rebar snipper to keep me away from him. She would leap down from his arm, and, because her wings were clipped, she would get on the floor and stretch her neck up until she looked like a small pink Big Bird as she charged me, screaming and hopping across the carpet as I tried to escape into a different room. She would grab my pants or my skirt with her beak and swing around, screaming and scolding. I had a lot of clothes with holes in them during that time.

Coral was my first and only large bird. I'd had small parrots before, but Coral was a much bigger project in many ways. As I've said, she bonded with my husband, but she grew more and more aggressive toward me and, to a lesser degree, toward my sons, who were just little kids at the time. The boys had the sense not to mess with her after a while. I wasn't so smart—and, besides, someone had to feed her and clean her very large cage every day.

A large parrot can break your fingers with her beak, and Coral frequently tried to break mine. She easily bent stainless steel spoons with that beak, and she could open Brazil nuts—those tough-shelled nuts that most people leave at the bottom of the bag

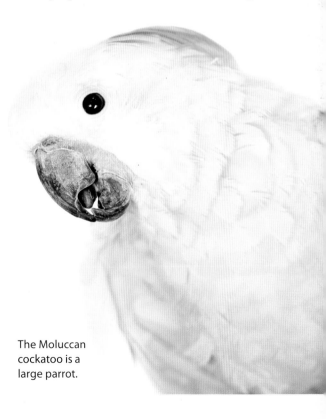

The Moluccan cockatoo is a large parrot.

of mixed nuts rather than trying to crack them. Her face was built for breaking stuff like that. She once pierced a tin can to get at the Le Sueur baby peas inside. They were her favorite treat, and she liked only that brand. I still have a numb area and a small scar on my thumb from one of the times she bit me. I remember leaning over the sink, teeth clenched and in tears, with my husband looking over my shoulder as my blood poured down the drain. Neither of us said a word. That bite happened in the mid-1990s.

This was back in the early days of the Internet and before I studied the science of behavior. As Coral became increasingly aggressive, I scoured early versions of online social media, such as AOL and Prodigy, for answers.

Somehow—miraculously—I located two professional parrot trainers, Doug Cook and Linda Morrow, a couple who worked primarily with parrots but also trained a variety of exotic animals, on an old listserv discussion group called rec.pets. birds. They were far ahead of the training curve at the time and had been training with clickers and treats for years before Karen Pryor popularized the technique among pet trainers in the 1980s. Karen had begun training dolphins in the 1960s, and before her were Marian and Keller Breland, Bob Bailey, and, of course, the great psychologist Burrhus Frederick Skinner, among others. Cook and Morrow advised me to read Pryor's book, *Don't Shoot the Dog*, and I was captivated by this new understanding that there are effective ways to change behavior.

Behavior is interesting, y'all! The only animal-training method I knew of before that time was the old-school force-based training that remains frustratingly popular today. As a teenager, I became briefly interested in training my family's purebred Scottish Terrier, and I even showed her in conformation once. I knew people who trained their dogs using corrections, but I wasn't interested in training my dog that way, so I moved on to other interests.

And then came Coral. You can't exactly put a choke chain on a parrot and pop the leash without either being attacked or killing the bird. Linda Morrow introduced me to another trainer, Melinda Johnson, who coached me completely by e-mail through the process of training this bird to accept me, to use her beak gently on my skin, and, ultimately, to do a lot of adorable tricks without my ever forcing her into anything. It worked. Coral changed her mind about me.

The technique I learned then is different from what I write about in this book, but what I learned to do with Coral was fundamentally a constructional approach. Johnson taught me to not even focus on Coral's aggressive behaviors. I was aware of them, of course, but I focused on rewarding anything she did that was not aggressive. A great many training techniques used by modern trainers are constructional in nature. CAT, which I will describe in this book, is about building desirable behavior rather than destroying bad behaviors.

Johnson also taught me to manage my parrot's access to my skin by initially training only when she was secured inside her cage. She advised me not to let Coral have a chance to bite so that she couldn't practice it and get better at it as well as to arrange Coral's environment in a way that would help her do the right things. From the time I started working on Coral's aggression, I didn't touch her for about two months. Because my husband was Coral's favorite, and she never bit him, she got plenty of time outside her cage each day with him for exercise, fun, and enrichment, but I took a break from handling her during her training.

I learned to train that parrot to do tricks for timely rewards instead of biting the living daylights out of me. With the advice of the generous trainers who worked with me, I helped Coral learn other ways to behave besides being dangerous and mean. Interestingly, in the process, I just taught her to do tricks on

A popular training method with dogs, clicker training is successful with many species of animal.

Dog trainers use shaping to teach cues and tricks.

cue rather than focusing on her aggression and thus built a fun relationship for us both. That's a little different from what I'll tell you about in this book, but some of the fundamentals were the same.

In training Coral, I learned about a training process called *shaping*, and this book will cover how we use shaping in CAT. The first thing I worked on with Coral was rewarding her for simply touching a stick gently. I used wooden chopsticks that I got in bulk at a dollar store because at first Coral just snapped them in two. I was taught that if she bit the stick just a tiny bit more softly than the previous time, even if the stick still broke, give her a treat. (Le Sueur baby peas were her training treat because I knew she would work for them.) Then I was to wait until she bit it even more softly, maybe only cracking the stick instead of breaking it in two.

Gradually, gradually, bit by bit, I was able to hold out the target stick, and Coral would touch it ever so lightly with the tips of her powerful yet sensitive beak. I would give her a treat only for that, and I stopped giving her treats when she bit harder. Now she preferred to touch the stick softly because that was what caused me to give her the peas. Changing her behavior was a way she could control her world. It must be terribly frustrating for a brilliant creature like a parrot (or a dog) to have no control over its world. This kind of reinforcement training gave Coral some of the control back.

The success I was able to achieve with this bird—that could eventually dunk a toy basketball, put baby socks in a tiny laundry basket, and put toys in a little wagon that she pulled, and that stopped causing cascades of blood to run down my arm and instead snuggled against me and coated me with her feather dust—made me hungry for more information about behavior and behavior analysis. *Don't Shoot the Dog* was a precious foundation, and despite the fact that many books on positive-reinforcement training are available today, I still recommend this book to anyone who wants a solid basis for understanding training and behavior.

I read what little animal-related writing I could find in the popular literature of the time, but much of it advocated punitive measures, so I found it of little interest. After all, I had taught an aggressive parrot to show me affection without any force, so I knew it didn't have to be that way. I moved on to reading textbooks. It wasn't long before I realized that I couldn't learn all I wanted to know without instruction from experts.

Through that old listserv, I met a member of the royal family of animal training. Her name was Marian Keller Bailey. She was a student of the famous psychologist B.F. Skinner back in the 1940s. She left the psychology program at the University of Minnesota and started Animal Behavior Enterprises (ABE) with her first husband, Breland Keller. This gutsy move happened during the Great Depression, a time when many people didn't have work and were struggling[1]. Starting such a seemingly frivolous venture at such a time was risky, but those two crazy kids saw the potential of the animal behavior technologies they had discovered in Skinner's labs. They launched and ran a successful business, training hundreds of animals for TV, movies, theater, the military, county fairs, and kids' birthday parties. I saw their Bird Brain exhibits in action at the Oklahoma State Fair in Blackwell when I was five years old; these included chickens and ducks that performed tricks such as pulling a chain to turn on a light before pecking the keys on a piano in exchange for a bit of food that dropped out when the task was completed. I didn't put two and two together for forty years until Bob Bailey (Keller Bailey's second husband)

---

1   Peterson, G.B. (2001). *The Clicker Journal: The Magazine for Animal Trainers*. Issues 49 & 50 (July/August/September/October), pp. 14 - 21.

was visiting the University of North Texas and showed pictures of it in a presentation. One of those Bird Brain boxes is at the Smithsonian now.

After reading my online posts that expressed my desire to study animal behavior, Marian Keller Bailey e-mailed me and told me that if I wanted to learn more about animal behavior, there was a highly respected Department of Behavior Analysis at the University of North Texas. She said the best thing to do was try to get into that program to study with Dr. Jesús Rosales-Ruiz. This was my sixth university attempt, but this time it stuck. I finished my Bachelor of Science degree in applied behavior analysis at the age of forty-seven and my Master of Science in behavior analysis at fifty.

One day, after I became a student again, I was sitting in a meeting of the Organization of Reinforcement Contingencies with Animals (ORCA) research lab, led by the man who would become my graduate thesis professor, Dr. Jesús Rosales-Ruiz (a.k.a. Dr. Rosales). I had planned to conduct my graduate research with parrots, but something else was on the horizon. Dr. Rosales asked the roomful of mostly twenty-somethings if anyone would be interested in performing research using the constructional approach with aggressive dogs.

Only one hand went up. It was that of a middle-aged fluffy woman who had gone back to college and lost her mind. That day, I signed on to intentionally come face-to-face with aggressive dogs again and again for years to come. My experience in training dogs and understanding their body language was quite minimal at the time. But this was interesting, and I was in it. It turned out to be one of the most gratifying things I've ever done.

There are quite a few people in the animal-training world who worked with animals in ways that are similar to what I will write about in this book long before Dr. Rosales and I conducted this specific

DID YOU KNOW?

Remember Ross Perot? Bob Bailey told me that he and Marian Keller Bailey used to do birthday parties for the Perot kids that featured a variety of trained animals, including pigs in racing silks, running around a track.

research. This book is not intended to claim that Dr. Rosales or I own the behavioral principle described by the research—that would be like Newton (or one of his students) claiming to have invented gravity. This approach is a natural way of learning. Instead, what Dr. Rosales did, and is still doing, and what several other research assistants and I have been fortunate enough to participate in, is digging into a deeper understanding of this natural process through experimentation so that people with real-world problems can have some tools to use in solving them. Dr. Rosales has also engaged the expertise of numerous trainers other than his students—dog trainers, zoo trainers, horse trainers, pet owners, and more—to explore the science of behavior. Granted, he knows a lot of really exceptional people (you know who you are).

I wrote this book with pet owners and their trainers in mind. With Dr. Rosales, I spent a few years traveling and teaching trainers and behaviorists about CAT. We taught across the United States, in Canada, in the United Kingdom, and in other places, both together and separately. As we did this work, I realized that we were not focusing enough on the most essential audience: the people who love these aggressive dogs; the ones who share their time, homes, and hearts with them; the ones to whom they snuggle close when the scary world is locked outside. This book is for you and your dog. I hope it will help you understand your canine friend and play a part in guiding you to the best decisions for your dog and for your family.

With the procedure I'll describe in the chapters that follow, we have developed a technology based on the laws of nature that can be used by trainers, behaviorists, and pet owners to replace pets' problem behaviors with safe, friendly ones in the environments where they live and spend their time. One of those long-ago listserv trainers, Doug Cook, was the first person I knew of to use such a procedure, although I didn't recognize what he was describing until some time after he passed away.

He explained how he worked with untamed parrots by approaching them in their enclosures. He would come to a distance that was almost too close for the bird's comfort but not so close that the bird would completely freak out in fear, a place that dog trainers call the *threshold*.

Cook would patiently wait, and as soon as he saw the bird doing things that he knew from experience meant that it felt calmer, such as shaking out its feathers, stretching a leg or wing out behind it, or preening its shoulder feathers, he would move away.

Because the birds were initially afraid of him, his departure was a reward. They would do more of whatever they had been doing when he went away. We don't usually think of rewards that way. We usually think of rewards as giving something, such as treats or petting or praise. But when the animal views the person as scary or threatening, the best reward of all, from the animal's point of view, is the person's going away. Doug rewarded slightly less fearful behavior, bit by bit, until the birds learned they could control him with their desirable behavior. After a while, these

birds stopped worrying so much and learned to trust him.

Dr. Rosales has a friend and colleague named Alexandra Kurland. She is an exceptional horse trainer and the author of several books about working with horses, mostly by using a clicker. Along with Dr. Rosales, she is a regular presenter at Karen Pryor's ClickerExpo. Kurland's work with horses was inspirational to him and played an influential role in this stream of research. One of Dr. Rosales's former students, Dr. Eduardo Fernandez, told me about when they were training at the Frank Buck Zoo in Gainesville, Texas, a small facility that had some sheep and goats who were supposed to be part of a petting zoo. Unfortunately, the animals had become aggressive. It was a tough case. When Fernandez (a master's student at the time) learned of Kurland's work, he

Positive reinforcement works with dogs of all sizes.

ran into Dr. Rosales's office, exclaiming, "Jesús! Jesús! I know what we need to do with them!" And so they conducted and collected data on a procedure similar to what Doug Cook had done with those birds, only with data collection and precision. And it worked.

In horse work, there is often pressure and release involved in the training: apply some pressure and then release it when the horse does what you want. A key element of Kurland's technique is that the pressure she applies isn't extreme or painful, as much horse training still is today. (People tend to default to force and pain in training because it seems quicker, but there are better ways.)

Kurland very skillfully sets up training environments so that the horses have the freedom to learn. They are not cranked around by the bits in their mouths, nor are they chased in a round pen. They are given opportunities to offer behaviors instead of being forced to do things, which gives them that important sense of control. The trainer reinforces (makes stronger) tiny increases in desirable behavior, either with distancing or acquisition of something they like, and more and more desirable behavior begins to happen. This makes all the difference in the world in how readily animals learn and what, specifically, they end up learning. Do they learn to cooperate in avoidance of pain, or do they learn that they have control in this training game and don't need to be defensive and afraid?

Just like with Coral, we have to give them managed control. That's how we'll garner their buy-in. That's how they'll learn to cooperate with us in learning socially acceptable and safe ways to behave.

When we collaborate with animals instead of forcing them, and when we give them choices and control within safe parameters, we can often change aggression into friendliness. Can we save every aggressive dog? No. Sometimes there is too much risk involved. Is working with aggressive dogs something that can be done without risk? No. Can we take euthanasia off the table in the discussion of canine aggression? I'm sorry to say that I do not believe we can. But sometimes we can find other choices for some dogs when we understand their aggression and when we can manage their environments in ways that change their minds about how they need to behave to feel safe in their world.

I began managing animal behavior programs at a Texas animal shelter in 2008. I've seen many animals that were simply too dangerous to put into homes. If they have already caused severe injuries, if they default to biting hard when things aren't going their way, if they are so powerful that no one can handle them, if they get riled up and can't calm back down, we have to consider all of these factors when determining whether to train, perform behavior modification, rehome, use some combination of these, or euthanize. It's a very difficult and haunting decision to be faced with. If you are like me and believe we should be

doing everything in our power to reduce the euthanasia of shelter animals, you should also understand that the people making these decisions are weighing the possibility of rehabilitating the dog, the dog's history of causing harm, the potential for him to cause harm again (possibly worse than before), and, sadly, the numbers of other dogs that may be healthy and friendly and adoptable right now but who may need to be euthanized at an animal shelter simply due to homelessness if all of the shelter's resources are invested in dangerous dogs. No one makes that decision lightly.

Most dog trainers say that pet owners should never work with their dog's aggression without a trainer's help. In fact, many dog trainers do not work with aggressive dogs at all. I can't blame them. It's risky and sometimes heartbreaking work. Sometimes it is true that you shouldn't try to work with your dog's aggression alone, so it may sound contrary that I'm telling you how to do this work.

But the fact is that you are already managing your dog and his behavior in some way, aren't you? You know him best. You love him best. If you learn more about how behavior works and how to manage your dog, maybe you'll learn enough to deal with this problem. A dog has the greatest chance of successful rehabilitation when he has a family who loves him and is committed to working with him. Even in the awful situations when a much-loved pet dog must be humanely euthanized for the safety of his family and community, would you prefer that a trainer, an animal-control facility, or I—people who are strangers to your dog—made that decision?

I'll walk you through the process of deciding what you can do, and I will explain how to do it, but, in the long run, you are the one who has to do most of the work. I'm going to talk honestly with you in this book, and I will give you my views. I hope that no matter what decisions you eventually make, this discussion will help you find the best possible solution for your dog.

Dogs that display reactive or aggressive behaviors pose different levels of risk. A 10-pound dog with aggression can sometimes be managed more easily than a 100-pound dog with aggression, but dogs of all sizes can cause injury to humans and other pets. In this book, I'll talk a lot about safety. You must consider safety on a normal day when nothing special is going on, whether you have a perfect dog or a dog that has already bitten and spent time in quarantine, and you're afraid he'll bite again. You must consider safety when you're going on an outing, such as a walk or to the vet, and on days when you are conducting behavior modification training. If you are the owner of a dog—any dog— safety is not something you can ever neglect, for your own safety and liability, for the safety of your community, and for the safety and well-being of your dog.

Does the CAT procedure work? Yes. It's been demonstrated over and over again, and it is currently used by many trainers around the world with all of the species I mentioned and probably more. As I wrote previously, CAT was also used in various forms by many trainers whose names are unknown to me, and a few I was lucky enough to know, before we committed it to research. Since we conducted the CAT research, the procedure continues to be used, and it has even been imitated, given other names, and placed in other contexts. This was hurtful at first, but now it's flattering. One of the things Dr. Rosales said when we first started our work—and repeated many times during the years I

was his student and later his colleague— was that the procedure is not something anyone should try to own; instead, it is something to teach to everyone interested enough to learn. No one owns the principles of behavior, but we've learned something about how they work. The reason we can confidently say that the CAT procedure can be used effectively is that it is based on scientific principles of behavior that have been backed up by research. But my goal here is to set aside the jargon and talk to you about what to do when you have a fierce dog. I hope that what I share here can help your family, your clients, your neighbors, and, most of all, you and your dog.

In my life and work during and since my participation in this research, I've had a lot of experiences with aggressive dogs. As a result, I may write some things in this book based on my own experiences that are my opinions and not direct results of the research and do not reflect the opinions of Dr. Rosales. If there are any factual errors, they are mine, not those of Dr. Rosales or Fox Chapel Publishing.

1

AGGRESSION AND THE CONSTRUCTIONAL AGGRESSION TREATMENT

> **It would not be amiss to point out that [Cujo] always tried to be a good dog.**
>
> **~ Stephen King**

Riley[1] originally belonged to next-door neighbors of the people I knew as his family. He was about a year old when his first family moved away and left him behind, all alone, in the backyard. He was thought to be a Doberman mix, but I kind of wondered if he might be an Australian Kelpie. It doesn't really matter. He was Riley. His kind neighbors realized he had been abandoned and took him in. He was a good dog with them. He was gentle with their adolescent son and quite agreeable with his new family. They quickly fell in love with him.

Within a week, however, he lunged and growled at someone while on a walk with his new mom. They also soon realized that he wasn't at all nice to people who entered their home. They took to crating him when they expected company. One time, a friend came early for a gathering at their home while Riley was loose in the house. She knocked on the door, and, without hearing a response, she entered and carried a casserole into the kitchen. These were,

after all, friends who were expecting her arrival. Riley promptly and loudly pinned this terrified woman in the kitchen. She was a cat person and not confident around dogs in general, so the whole event had an extra layer of scariness. The family was able to pull Riley away, and he did not hurt the guest, but it was a concerning situation and not the only time Riley did that sort of thing.

Riley was eleven years old when I met him. That's pretty old for a pretty big dog, but he was still agile and strong, and he lived for several more years. Like most dog families, this family loved their dog, and they were willing to make a lot of concessions for him. In addition to crating him when guests came over, they had only one option when they needed to board Riley: their vet's office. Riley didn't like the vet, but he did like one of the techs there, so they were able to board him when she was available. When I met with the family, they told me that if that particular tech wasn't available, the family would take separate vacations so that someone could stay at home with

---

1   Riley was a real dog, but this is not his real name. I've changed the names of the aggressive dogs to protect their families' privacy.

Lunging on the leash can be part of a dog's aggressive behavior.

Riley. This was useful information. It told me that he actually had been successful in making friends outside his immediate family. He also liked the grandmother, who visited once or twice year. But they were the only ones.

The goal for training Riley was to help him make more friends. His owner told me, "We just want him to be able to have friends. He doesn't have any friends but us." Maybe that wasn't important to Riley, but it was important to his family, and families matter, too. Families matter a lot[2].

It's hard to be the owner of a dog who doesn't like other people or animals, but it's even harder when the dog exhibits

aggressive displays and actions toward them. It makes for a frustrating and challenging life for the owners and has a significant impact on the whole family's quality of life—human and canine members alike. A lot of Rileys end up in shelters, and many are eventually euthanized because of their aggression when families just can't make it work. After working with a lot of these dogs, I understand that decision. It breaks my heart, but I usually support it. I feel deeply for those families.

I was pretty naïve when it came to working with aggressive dogs at the time I began working on CAT. I was used to parrots and cats. But it didn't really matter. I didn't work with dogs, per se. I was working with their behavior. It sounds like an unnecessary distinction, I'm sure, but behavior works in certain ways across all species, and it is those

---

2   It's easy for trainers and behaviorists to put the dog first in our behavior-modification plans because that's where our expertise is. Most of us don't get training in counseling human families, but we should. A dog-behavior professional sees your dog for only a few brief sessions, and then we hand the leash back to you. As the owner of an aggressive or reactive dog, you are vastly important in the process. It cannot work without you.

Whether with your phone or a video camera, be ready to record your dog's training.

principles of behavior that we were studying in the research. In this book, you are going to learn how to study your dog's behavior.

We didn't have a lab full of aggressive dogs to study at the University of North Texas, but families looking for help with their aggressive dogs were easy to find. Dr. Rosales often guides his students through working with animals in their homes, and that is what happened with me. Most of the dogs I worked with lived with families. A few lived in animal shelters. The way the research went was that I would go to pet owners' homes or meet them in spaces where aggression was known to occur, and I worked with the dogs in their real worlds. In every case, I either set up a video camera on a tripod or had someone videotape what we did. I recorded the work I did with every dog. This was in the early 2000s before everyone had good cameras inside their easily portable smartphones. You probably won't have to buy a new piece of equipment to record your work, but make sure your phone is charged.

After each session, I took the videos back to Dr. Rosales's office to view them and discuss what went wrong and what went right, what else I might try, what to leave out, and what to add to what I was doing. We met every Wednesday at 2:00 p.m. (I called these my "come to Jesús" meetings). Obsessive video recording and watching every video with your professor is a very effective way to get over your fear of seeing yourself on tape. The videotapes were extremely useful, so the embarrassment I sometimes felt was worth it.

IMPORTANT!

Before I go any further, I caution you: Do not try any of the stuff I'm going to tell you about until you've finished reading the whole book and until you have painstakingly determined that you are up to the task of keeping everyone safe as you do the work. You and others can get hurt while working with aggressive or reactive dogs. If a voice in the back of your head is saying, "I can't do this alone," listen to it. If you hear that voice, find and work with a cooperative trainer who will read this book.

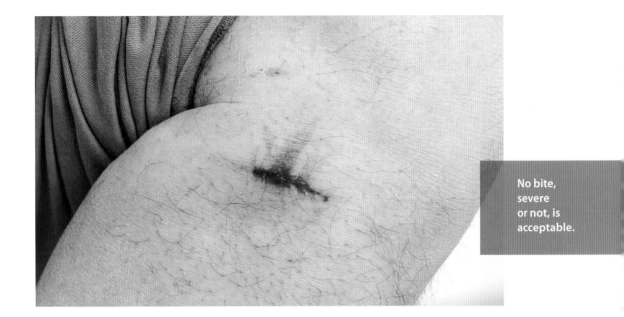

To my great fortune, very little went wrong in terms of safety during my work on the procedure. I was bitten once by a large mixed-breed dog named Max, and ten years later I was bitten by a German Shepherd Dog named Gunther. I regret both of these events deeply, and not just because of the injuries I sustained—very minor with Max, thanks to my heavy sweatshirt, and worse but not life-threatening with Gunther; I will always have a scar to remind me.

I confess that the bite from Max was totally my fault. I wasn't paying enough attention to the husband, who was handling the dog, or to the dog himself. I was explaining something to the wife, who was in front of me, and I happened to glance down at the dog to my left. Max was much closer to me than he had been a moment before. He was staring hard at me from close range. The husband was holding the leash loosely. I made the briefest of eye contact with Max before he launched himself upward at me. I raised my arm to block the dog's lunge toward my face. My favorite sweatshirt got a bite taken out of it, and I got a bruised wrist but no broken skin. It could have been much worse.

If you want to work with your aggressive dog, you have to pay attention. Distraction is not acceptable, and I was distracted. The incident you suffer might not be to your wrist. What if I had not looked down just then? He would have gone for my neck or face. You can tell where a dog is going to bite by where he is staring, and he wanted my head.

With Gunther, it is not as clear to me what happened. I still ponder it, but the best advice I can give myself is that I should have worked slower. When in doubt, take a break, watch your videos, and think it through. On that particular day, I wanted to work up to at least the point we had gotten to in our previous session, but Gunther wasn't up for it.

Very little went wrong in terms of developing the CAT procedure; we just kept tweaking and adjusting. It was incomplete at first, but as we built it up, it got better and better. Under Dr. Rosales's guidance, I had success after success working with these dogs. I do not take credit other than to say that I followed instructions and had a very good instructor. In the process, I learned how to observe well so I could understand what I was seeing and act accordingly.

When working with Riley, I took my then-eighteen-year-old son along as my videographer for the first session. I worked with Riley's family for a couple of hours the first day, but I actually performed CAT for only forty-five minutes. Some in the popular dog-training world had gotten the misconception that CAT takes too long, but I'll take forty-five minutes any day for a successful first aggression behavior-modification session. Since then, I've had a successful first session in only thirty minutes. We have more work to do after that, but it's a really good start. All humane behavior-modification techniques for aggression take time. To be honest, it was not common to have this kind of very quick success in such a short session, but it wasn't unheard of, either. But most sessions take longer.

There are other techniques that can work quickly, but they are risky and send you away with way too many problems; these include using shock collars,

Along with being painful to the dog, a shock collar can worsen aggressive behavior.

dangling the dog from his collar until he passes out, pinning the dog to the floor—I'm sorry to say that these antiquated and dangerous techniques are still in use today in the United States, and they have a very high probability of making the dog worse, making him harder to read, and taking away his warning signals, which can result in someone getting badly hurt. To be blunt, these methods are unethical and inhumane. In some countries, they are against the law, but in the United States, you can see them on TV shows.

The people who use, teach, and promote these harsh techniques also have a different definition of "what works." For them, the dog doesn't have to like the situation, he just has to shut down and do nothing except follow orders when he's feeling afraid or defensive. That is not good enough for me, and that is not how I define what works. Our goal with CAT and the goals of other modern, effective trainers—whether or not CAT is their preferred behavior-modification procedure—is to change

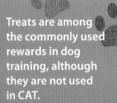

Treats are among the commonly used rewards in dog training, although they are not used in CAT.

the dog's viewpoint from one of terrible fear and defensiveness to one of peaceful confidence. The harsh techniques I mentioned can work to eliminate aggression if they are performed when and only when the problem behavior occurs so that the dog knows what to do to consistently prevent the negative reinforcement from happening, and when to do it. But these techniques are very likely to produce a sneakier dog who will act calm until he gets easy access to someone he can bite.

You cannot use harsh techniques if you want a safe, happy dog. No one is happy when his or her life is full of waiting for the next shock. If you shock a dog at the wrong millisecond, you can zap the good behavior instead of the bad. And if you shock a dog when another dog or a human is nearby, the dog can learn that the shock and the other dog or human are a

package deal, so the next time he sees a dog or human, he may interpret the shock as a cue to attack to protect himself—even if the dog or human are simply innocently walking or happen to be in the aggressive dog's proximity. It becomes like a superstition for the aggressive dog: "If I see a stranger, I will feel a shock, because that other time I saw a stranger, I felt a shock." The "shock" can be an actual shock, a leash jerk with a prong collar, a hit from his owner, or nearly any other situation that the dog doesn't like.

The scientifically proven, effective, and humane techniques take time. That said, I sometimes get relatively fast results using CAT. One unstudied possible reason seems to be working as much as I can in one day. I schedule a day with the owner and the team we need to work

with, and we work together for several hours. We stock up on water and snacks for ourselves and the dogs, and we take some breaks, but we keep working for a few hours. When you work for thirty minutes or an hour here and there, you'll see progress, but you're going to need more sessions, and with each additional session, you're going to lose a little ground and then regain some ground. Each time, you'll be exposing the dog to many things you didn't necessarily plan for, such as different weather, the different outfit you're wearing, the new helper dog you're using, and anything else that has changed since the last time you worked together. There is nothing wrong with that, and, in our busy lives, that is often what we have to work with. But if you want to get more done, my bet is that you'll do better if you train longer at each session.

CAT shows your dog how to live safely in his world with the kind of activity that is going to go on for the rest of his life. The advantage to long sessions, especially at first, is that you may make more significant progress earlier. There are drawbacks, obviously. First, it's expensive if you're doing this with a dog trainer (so are all the other techniques, which is one reason trainers schedule shorter sessions). A trainer who works with aggressive dogs tends to charge more per session because they need more liability insurance, they are putting themselves at greater risk, and there are simply fewer trainers who will work with aggressive dogs, so they are responding to the market's demand for their services. Trainers who specialize in aggression tend to stay pretty busy, but it's hard, exhausting, and often draining work.

When you have an aggressive dog, management techniques are essential. Management refers to how you hold the leash, confine the dog when company comes over, distract him from things to which he might respond aggressively, and a variety of other measures that you take to prevent him from behaving badly. This is often the lion's share of what a trainer works on with owners because it's very important to be able to prevent problems from happening. That's why I thought it was so necessary to write a book that talks to owners. You're going to do the bulk of the work. You need to understand it.

There are some short procedures you can do now, whenever a problem comes up, no extensive training needed. Chances are, you're already doing some of them. For example, say you're on a walk, and you see a strange dog at the end of the street that you know your dog will charge toward if he gets a chance. In a case like that, if your dog hasn't seen the other dog yet, you can just smoothly turn around and go in another direction to avoid the problem altogether. There's no harm in that, and much benefit. That's management. Manage the situation so your dog doesn't get a chance to react aggressively, or, if he does, you can control his behavior safely.

If your dog is known to be aggressive to people and dogs while on walks, plan your walks for times when few other people are

How will you manage a dog who guards a spot on the furniture?

out with their dogs. Put in some work with your dog before you start trying to walk him on leash in the neighborhood after dinner on a beautiful day when everyone is out with their dogs. Or, better yet, if possible, exercise your dog in your safely fenced backyard until he's ready for a slightly more challenging situation. That's not the CAT procedure, it's just avoiding trouble when you can. It's both necessary and smart.

What do you do when your dog has already spied the other dog and is stiffening, growling, or starting to lunge? If the other dog is heading the other direction, just stand and wait until your dog does anything less threatening, even if only for a second, and then casually turn and walk away in another direction. Yes, as long as your dog is not overstimulated, I suggest that you let him watch the other dog until he decreases his aggressive behavior. Only do this if the other dog is far enough away that your dog can calm himself enough to do something besides behaving aggressively.

For training sessions, you will set up a learning environment and minimize distractions like other dogs showing up on the horizon. If the other dog or person is too close, and your dog is losing his cool, all you can do is cut your losses. Get your dog to a safe place and, if needed, tell the other person that your dog is in training and ask him or her to back off. "Stop! My dog is in training!" Chances are, this will set your training back and you'll have to redo some of the work you've already done, but that's just how it is. It's a lot better than letting the other person or dog approach and having your dog hurt them.

Head turning and/or yawning are neutral behaviors that you can reward.

It's also less stressful for your dog to leave the situation rather than going into full-out attack mode.

My son, the cameraman during my work with Riley, followed me through the steps of approaching Riley and walking away when he behaved a little bit better than before. We did this back-and-forth for forty-five minutes, only walking away when Riley either turned away from me, sat, yawned, snapped at a fly instead of at me, sniffed toward me, tipped his head to the side, barked less threateningly—anything that was a little bit friendlier and safer than the previous time. At first, you have to take what you can get—like the dog snapping at a fly—reward the behavior, and then see if the dog offers something a little better in the next setup. Snapping at a fly is actually a pretty good alternative behavior. When Riley did that, it meant that he was not obsessively focusing on chasing me away anymore. He'd calmed down enough that he could tend to the pesky fly, and that was something I reinforced.

Interestingly, when we experimented with where and when Riley would behave aggressively, he did not behave aggressively toward me when we were outside on the front sidewalk, although he did with some other people at other times. He didn't bark or growl when I walked up the sidewalk, although that was one of his modus operandi. He didn't even bark when I walked right up to the door. But when I got a foot in the door, all hell broke loose.

This preliminary information is important to know. Aggression is always situation-specific. Your dog does not always behave aggressively toward everyone at all times, does he? It's rare for a family to keep a dog who reacts badly to everyone, family and stranger alike. So we want to find the situations in which your dog behaves this way. This is where you'll start working with him, if possible.

At the beginning of the forty-five minutes with Riley and his owner, I could not enter the house. Riley would lunge and charge from the living room, where his owner held onto his leash for dear life. Riley meant business. At the end of that forty-five minutes, I knelt beside him and he approached (still on a leash held by his owner) and nestled his head under my arm with a wiggly, happy body and leaned into me. I followed this up by letting my son approach him. After all, he had been part of the work we had just done, so it was kind of a two-for-one deal. Riley accepted him in just the same way he had accepted me.

His owner said, "Riley, you have a new friend! You have two new friends!" That was a big deal. I have really warm feelings for a lot of difficult dogs because they softened up through the process of our work together, and they eventually let me, my assistant, or my dog be their friend. Riley was one of them.

But, there's something else you need to know. You're not done after just one successful training session. Working with aggression is not a one-and-done

Your training goal may be to make your dog more comfortable in public.

proposition. I get a lot of calls from people asking for a few tips to help with a dog's aggression. Over the phone. And, by the way, the family doesn't really want to change what they're already doing. This won't work.

Rehabilitating a dog with aggression is not a quick fix. It requires that you change a lot of what you are doing. And it requires that you work with your dog repeatedly and in different situations.

For your next session, you're going to change up your training environment a little. Now, instead of you holding the dog's leash, you might have your well-instructed spouse or someone else your dog trusts hold it. Ideally, the person will have read this book first; if not, you have to make sure you instruct the person and

that he or she follows your instructions. Once your dog is OK with letting someone approach him, you'll introduce a stranger or a different dog. Once that person or dog becomes a friend, you'll need to change the location. You might start over in the backyard after the living room has become a safe place. Or maybe go to the edge of the park, away from where everyone likes to be, and do a session there. Or go to a different room in the house.

This is called *generalization*. Steve White[3] is an instructor for police dog trainers who says that good generalization for a working dog like his requires introducing the dog to fifty different people, fifty different places, and fifty

---

3   Steve is a police officer, and he uses nonaversive techniques to get the best, most reliable behaviors out of his working dogs. His website is www.proactivek9.com.

different situations to do each behavior he's being taught. This way, the dog knows that he has the same control of all these environments and that the same rules apply. It's when you do that kind of generalization work that you're really going to see good results. If you do not have time to do that much generalization, do as much as you can and add new situations as often as possible. Understand that you're not done until the dog can handle all the situations that are important in your life, and, even then, you always have to pay attention.

You have to understand that when you start over in a new situation, the dog may act like you haven't trained him at all, even after he's been perfect in the first training situation for weeks. So make it easy for him. As Karen Pryor says in *Don't Shoot the Dog*, "Go back to kindergarten."

A very cool thing can happen in this part of the training. Often (although not always) the subsequent sessions in new situations are shorter, and then there can be a time when you'll see a light bulb come on over the dog's head. He starts to realize, *Hey, these new rules work just as well with short blonde women and with tall guys with beards and hats. They apply in the living room and when we're out walking in the neighborhood. They apply when I'm hungry and when I've just finished eating. When it's dark and when it's light.* And one day, a lot of these dogs figure out that the world isn't as scary as they thought. *All of these people and dogs will go away when*

I am nice, not only when I'm aggressive. (An important note here: You will always have to make sure that the world at large doesn't give your dog more than he can handle. That's another area in which you are going to have to stay on the job.)

Three weeks after Riley's training session in which we achieved friendship in forty-five minutes, I took a new assistant along with me to Riley's house. When Riley saw me, he grinned and wiggled and greeted me happily right from the start. He remembered me. When he saw my new assistant, all bets were off. We started the work from the beginning, and I gave her instructions. We worked for twenty minutes, and then Riley approached, let her pet him, took a treat from her, and let her walk him by his leash. His body was soft, his grin was wide, and his tail was gently wagging.

Although they did it completely by accident, preventing Riley from meeting a lot of strangers was probably one of the best things the owners could have done for him. Dogs that get a lot of exposure to things that worry them learn to behave aggressively in many different situations. The common advice that dogs need socialization isn't exactly accurate because most people, including some trainers, don't understand what socialization is. People think that taking a dog out and exposing him to a lot of things is all there is to it, but if the dog is already reactive, or if the dog is overwhelmed during the experience, it can be detrimental.

Dogs benefit from the right things done in the name of socialization. Puppies should be exposed to friendly dogs and friendly people who follow instructions in safe, fun situations. But they should not be exposed to twenty-five strange dogs at a dog park to help them get over reactivity to dogs or to a party of raucous people and loud music to help them become less reactive to people. Dogs' behavior can be damaged and rendered even more difficult to fix if they are overexposed to things that worry, frighten, or overwhelm them, especially as young pups. For them, these experiences will build much of the foundation on which the rest of their life experiences will rest.

Socializing adult dogs is completely different from socializing puppies. Your adult dog has already been acclimated to some things in life. In animal shelters, we get many dogs who come from hoarding cases. Such a dog may have lived in a 1,000-square-foot mobile home with fifty other dogs, mounds of feces, and a scarce food supply. Seriously. It happens all the time. These dogs are socialized. They are just socialized to unhealthy situations. They're socialized to large numbers of other dogs, all of whom are living in the same unhealthy conditions, and sometimes they have to fight for food or defend themselves from bigger, stronger dogs. But they are socialized.

Usually, dogs from hoarding cases are not in great health because most people who have fifty dogs can't provide them with adequate care. And they aren't socialized to live comfortably with people. Most hoarders are single, older people, usually women, who live with all the animals they can collect and the offspring of those animals, and their offspring, and so on. The hoarders often have mental or emotional disorders that prevent them from understanding that the animals they own are not receiving appropriate care, despite their love for the animals. So, as you can see, if you bring home a dog that is socialized to living in a hoarding situation, that's not what we mean when we say dogs should be socialized. If your dog is socialized in a dog park where out-of-control dogs bully him, that's the wrong kind of socialization, too.

Don't take your dog-aggressive or people-aggressive dog to the dog park. Your dog does not need to meet random dogs. He needs to feel safe. Being around a bunch of dogs does not make a dog-

Left: Play is a normal part of puppies' socialization.

Below: Some dogs welcome interaction with new people, but it's never advised to put your face near an unfamiliar dog's face.

aggressive dog feel safe. Even if he does well with his training and gets to the point where he can be around some dogs under supervision for short periods of time, just one bad experience at the dog park will mess up his training and could send you back to the beginning, or it could make your dog's behavior worse than what you started out with.

Dog-reactive dogs don't need dog parks; they need empty spaces, like your fenced backyard. A dog park also is not a suitable place for a puppy in need of socialization because one bad dog in that park can damage your puppy's behavior, injure his body, or even kill him. And it's definitely not the place for a dog who already has social issues.

Don't require your dog to greet strangers until he's learned that meeting strangers is a fun thing to do. Some dogs don't like being touched much, so,

for them, a greeting from a distance is plenty and will always be enough. When your dog is ready, introduce him only to nice people who will follow your instructions and to dogs you know and trust. Don't do this at a party. Invite one or two people over at a time and let them know that you have certain rules. If they don't follow the rules, crate the dog in a separate area.

I have a dog-loving friend who is just as nice as can be, but she wouldn't listen to me when I was trying to teach a puppy not to jump on people. She would tell me, "It's OK! She just wants to say hi. You have to let her be a puppy!" Well, what if I, as the owner, don't want her jumping on everyone? I get to decide for my puppy, and you get to decide for your dog. Even if you know that someone is kind and responsive to your instructions, don't let anyone touch your dog unless your dog invites it and you approve it. Only approve it if you are 99.9% sure that your dog will be OK with it.

Instead of allowing people to handle your dog in their own ways, assuming your dog is safe to handle, you can say, "Well, let's see what he says first." Then describe the body language you're seeing. "See how he's turning his head and you can see the whites of his eyes? And how he's trying to go the other way? That tells me that he doesn't want to say hi right now." (This applies to every dog, not just aggressive ones.) If your dog's body language tells you that he is uncomfortable to any degree, stop the interaction. Just say, "We're going to finish up our walk now. Talk to you later!" And if that doesn't work, say, "My dog has had enough time out for one day, so I'm going to get him home before he gets overwhelmed."

If you approve an interaction with your dog who is just learning to accept new people, make the person keep it short. Let Fido decide who he wants to be touched by and then quickly call him away and give him a treat. Don't stand and talk for thirty minutes with your neighbor with your reactive dog in training on leash beside you. If you want to talk with your neighbor, invite her over or ask her to be part of your training procedure. Don't ask your dog to do more than he is ready to do. It can backfire.

If your dog is already behaving aggressively, you know what your dog's aggression looks like, or you wouldn't be reading this book, right? Now you need to learn what he does *before* he behaves aggressively. A lot of people think their dogs didn't give them any warning signals before they bit, but chances are they did, and the owners just didn't understand the body language the dogs were using. Or the owners weren't paying attention to the right things.

How does your dog tell you he's getting overwhelmed? You know what he looks like when he's lunging, but it's important for you to learn what he does before he lunges. Maybe his chain of behaviors is something like this: he sees a stranger, he freezes, he barks and then growls, he lunges, and then he bites (or tries to) and scares the bejeebers out of people, including you.

A friendly first meeting on a busy city street. Many dogs would be overwhelmed in this situation.

Ideally, when should you intervene? Not after he bites someone. You need to intervene when he first sees that stranger and starts to freeze. Or even earlier. What does he do when he even notices that another person is around? You have to be that much in tune with your aggressive dog.

As I was preparing to write this book, I asked my trainer friends on Facebook how they define *reactivity* and how they define *aggression*. These are essential terms in the aggressive-dog world. Do you know that each one of the two dozen people who responded defined them differently? Only one trainer defined these terms the way I use them. The good news is that they each had definitions they worked with.

There's a saying in dog training that the only thing two dog trainers can agree

on is that the third one is wrong. Part of the problem is that our language has turned into jargon. Dog-training jargon is worse than most because it originates in a variety of different places and is used by a lot of different communities. Jargon is just one of the many tricky things about learning how to treat canine aggression—or aggression in any species. And the information you'll find online is all over the map in terms of both jargon and validity.

If you talk to any two dog trainers, their definitions of aggression and reactivity might be different. If you pick up three different books by different trainers, you might read three different definitions, even if all of the trainers have basically the same training philosophy. For this reason, it's very important to ask people to define their

Aero, the author's dog, wears a gentle expression.

terms before you walk too deeply into a discussion.

One way—and in my view, the best way—to clear things up is to stick to descriptions of the behavior that the dog actually performs rather than using catch-all terms like *reactivity* and *aggression*. To describe a dog's behavior, watch him, see what he does, and make note of it. In other words, if you notice your dog "being aggressive," he is doing something that makes you label his behavior as "aggressive" in your mind. Aggression isn't a behavior you can measure, but a behavioral description might be something like this: "He looked at the other dog; his body got very still; he growled, lowered his head, backed up, and ran forward; and he bit Sal on her backside."

Aggression, along with other labels such as *fear*, *anxiety*, *timidity*, and so forth, are labels we use for collections of behaviors that we can see. If you say your dog was being aggressive, your spouse might say, "Oh, that wasn't aggression; he was just excited." But if you say, "He ran forward and bit Sal on the butt," the other person is more likely to agree that the dog's behavior wasn't friendly. You might even be able to prove it because Sal might have bite marks on her hind end.

Just last night, I was walking past my ottoman. Aero, my dog, was walking with me, and he jumped up on the ottoman just as my hand swung backward. As he jumped upward, his eyeball met my pinky finger straight on. He instantly made a fierce-sounding combination of a growl and a bark in my direction before rubbing his eye with his paw. I jumped back because it was obvious he was not saying, "I love you, Mom" in his moment of distress. He had been hurt, and I was there, and he reacted. That's how I define reactivity. Both his behavior ("gr-awr!") and mine (jumping away from him) were reactions. It could still be reactive behavior if he had been frightened or made uncomfortable without the pain of being poked in the eye.

If, for some crazy reason, I continued to poke him in the eye every time he jumped onto the ottoman, a couple of things might happen. One is that he might not jump up on the ottoman when I'm around. Another is that he might repeat that growl-bark, I might jump back again, and thus he might avoid getting poked in the eye. Either one of these connections, in his doggy mind, indicates that he is no longer merely reacting but that he has now learned how to avoid the negative outcome of being poked in the eye. He either simply avoids the situation by not jumping onto the ottoman, or he growl-barks, which makes me go away without poking him in the eye.

Reactivity occurs only the first few times it happens in a new situation. Beyond that, for the purposes of definition in this book, the behavior is called *aggression*. The behavior is not automatic; rather, the dog learned the behavior based on discovering what would happen if he did it (he growled, and I jumped back). By the time your dog's behavior has happened enough times to be a problem, it's not reactivity anymore. It's behavior that has paid off in the past, so he's going to do the same thing again. That's aggression.

Let's say there's a dog named Bob who went on his first walk in a new neighborhood, and a man approached him and his owner to say hello. The first time this happened, the dog growled. That may have been reactivity. But, suppose that as soon as the dog growled, the man walked away. The dog just found out that the noise he made actually benefitted him. He experienced that his growly behavior can change people's behavior. It doesn't matter if the man would have walked away anyway. The dog doesn't know that. The man went away, and that's exactly what the dog wanted.

Isn't that interesting? Because the dog wanted the man to go away, and the man did go away, the dog is now more likely

If this dog's barking results in a scary stranger leaving him alone, he is more likely to bark in the future.

to growl at people the next time he wants them to go away while out on walks. So, in the way I define it, that behavior has changed from reactivity to aggression.

Aggression is learned behavior. It may be noticeable but not look like much (such as simply staring at someone) until you learn what he's likely to do next. It may be severe, as in biting the snot out of the person. But the dog has learned that this behavior is an effective way to deal with problems in the world. This aggressive behavior is now learned growling[4], not reactive growling, and we'll use the label *aggressive* for all of the behaviors that a dog might perform in that context. Bob growls to get the man to go away. His growling works, and it produces something valuable to him: distance from things he's worried about.

At some point, you may find that someone (your vet, a trainer or behaviorist, or even your teenager who has been researching to find a solution to your dog's aggression) recommends medication for your aggressive dog. What I recommend is that you get your dog checked out by your vet to identify any health concerns. Even a condition that is not normally associated with aggressive behaviors may be related in the case of your individual dog. I once worked with a dog that had not seen a vet in nine years because his owner couldn't get him there due to the dog's aggressive behavior. The dog had huge, bulging eyeballs, which can

be associated with health concerns. Maybe the dog could have been treated nine years earlier, and his behavior could have been prevented from getting that bad, but we'll never know.

For your health visit, your vet may need to prescribe a mild sedative for your dog so that you are able to get your dog to the clinic. Alternatively, mobile vets are becoming more common. A mobile vet is a veterinary office on wheels that will simply pull up at your curb. You won't have to worry about running into other dogs and people with your dog.

Most people consult their veterinarians when they have any issues with their dogs, whether health, behavior, or diet. Veterinarians are not necessarily trained in behavior, although they might be. If you want your vet to be your primary consultant regarding your pet's behavior, ask what education and training he or she has had with respect to animal behavior. If you are lucky enough that your veterinarian is one of the few veterinary behaviorists certified by the American College of Veterinary Behaviorists (ACVB), he or she has specific training related to behavior. Veterinarians with thirty years of experience can probably handle any animal you put in front of them because of their experience, but it doesn't mean they are experts on how to create successful behavior-change programs. Veterinarians are essential professionals in the care of your dog, but ask questions when you talk with them about your dog's aggression. There are

---

4   Behavior analysts call this kind of learned behavior operant behavior because the behavior works on the environment to produce a desirable outcome for the dog.

A vet can sometimes modify how your dog is examined to make your dog more comfortable.

some amazing veterinarians out there. You may need to try a couple to find the one that works best for you and your dog.

Most of us don't like the idea of putting our pets on medication any more than we like the idea of being on it ourselves, but don't be too quick to dismiss it. Sometimes medication can be prescribed for a brief time to help you manage the intensity of your dog's aggression, and then you can wean the dog from the medication later as you continue the behavior-modification process. A few dogs may benefit from staying on the medication, and if your vet thinks it's a good idea, there's nothing wrong with that. If you and your vet together decide to wean the dog off the medication, you will need to continue with behavior modification as you reduce the medication because your dog may behave in some of his old ways when the effects of the medication are no longer present.

Talk to your veterinarian about how various medications may affect your dog's behavior and how your dog feels. There are some medications that are not recommended for dogs with aggression. Acepromazine (abbreviated as "ace"), for example, is a nervous-system depressant that reduces the observable behaviors your dog performs but does not change his emotional responses. It's sometimes referred to as *chemical restraint*. Ace has its place in veterinary medicine, but it will not teach a dog to behave less aggressively in the big scheme of things. It will only make him temporarily less able to do anything about whatever he is concerned about. Chemical restraint is not at all what we're looking for when we're trying to rehabilitate an aggressive dog.

Fortunately, there are several appropriate medications available that you can discuss with your veterinarian.

Many of them don't make your dog act doped-up or sleepy. As long as the dog can function well on the medication, and the veterinarian considers it appropriate, it can be a helpful approach for many dogs. You will need to monitor your dog and contact your vet if your dog's behavior suggests that he is not responding well to the medication. He may need a dose adjustment or even a different medication. Some of these kinds of drugs take weeks to show their full effectiveness, and even if they did take effect overnight, you would not see a suddenly well-behaved dog. Your dog will still need help with the behavioral component of the aggression. Medication is not a magic bullet, but for some cases of aggression, it is something that can get aggressive-dog owners over the hump more safely until they can perform behavior modification.

There are dogs that end up staying on medication long-term. If weaning off the medication, along with behavior

modification, is not working well, or if you are just happy with the way things are on the medication and your veterinarian approves, make the decision that works best for you and your pet.

If your vet doesn't want to consider medication, ask for his or her reasons, which may be related to the animal's overall health or the vet's philosophy regarding antianxiety meds for dogs. You can always get a second opinion from another vet, just as you would if you were dealing with your own health. You must be proactive when dealing with canine aggression. Sometimes a perfectly good vet is not perfectly right for your particular case.

Ensuring that your dog is healthy is extremely important when deciding how to deal with his aggression. Pain is a common reason for aggression. I used to have a Greyhound named Bravo who was just as lovely a dog as you could ever want to meet. She was sweet and friendly, and she loved

people of all shapes and sizes. She was my primary helper dog in the CAT research. But when she was eight years old, she began to get uncharacteristically grumpy. One day, I petted her while she was on her bed. I noticed a new bump I hadn't seen before and knelt to examine it. She snapped at my face. This was her first show of aggression. This was a dog that would let our small dog eat out of the same bowl with her (this was not the dogs' usual eating arrangement, and not one that I would recommend, but the little guy often tried to get into her food while she was eating, and it was never an issue). We assumed it was normal aging, aches and pains, and maybe some arthritis. It was winter, and she was nearly nine years old. Even a cold day in Texas can make old bones ache.

But one terrible day, Bravo stood up, and her back leg broke. It just broke. She screamed. I rushed her to the vet. She had osteosarcoma. Bone cancer. She was a gentle old dog who started behaving aggressively because she was in pain. If I had started treating her for aggression, I would have done her a terrible disservice. She needed a vet.

Thyroid problems are known to precipitate aggressive behavior, and so can less serious issues, like a tummy ache or a cold. All kinds of health issues can cause grouchiness that leads to aggression. When you don't feel well, you don't always act nicely. Health problems don't cause aggression, per se, but they do make it more valuable to the dog to be left alone.

So, in a situation where a healthy Fido would have greeted his owner with joy, a sick Fido might snap because he doesn't feel well and just wants to be alone.

Without treating health issues, any behavior work you do with your dog will be less effective or even completely ineffective. Learning doesn't work as well when the learner is under stress. At the first sign of a temperament change, check out the most obvious cause—health—first. The sooner the health problem is treated, the better. And the sooner the behavior problem is treated, the better.

All dogs should be examined by veterinarians before starting behavior modification for aggression. Consider looking for a Fear Free-certified vet in your area or asking your vet to become Fear Free certified. Fear Free vets have special training in handling techniques that can safely and humanely reduce the stress on animals in their care by adjusting how they touch the animals, how they arrange their clinics, and how they help prepare you for getting your dog from your home to the clinic and back home again with minimal stress. To find out if your vet is certified, or to find a Fear Free-certified vet in your area, visit www.fearfreepets.com.

Earlier, I told you that different trainers and behaviorists define the labels *reactivity* and *aggression* in many different ways. This is true. But when you ask them what dogs do when they are aggressive, you might hear similarities. After all, we've all been to a lot of the

A veterinary visit is your first step when your dog begins to behave aggressively.

same classes and have read the same books. Importantly, we've all watched a lot of dogs exhibiting a lot of behaviors.

By my definitions, the terms *reactive* and *aggressive* are just labels for groups of behaviors. Reactivity is a response that happens a few times and then either stops or continues because the dog has learned that his response effects some desired outcome, like chasing a scary person away. Aggression is behavior that happens because of the outcome it produces. So, it would seem that we just need to figure out how to get rid of the aggressive behaviors, right? Would it surprise you if I said no? What we need to figure out is not how to get rid of aggression, but what we want the dog to do instead of behaving aggressively.

In a seminar that Dr. Rosales and I presented in San Francisco, he talked about identifying significant behaviors for working with your dog. He said, "What does your dog do just before he bites? *That* is the important behavior." We're not necessarily looking for that predictable behavior chain of freeze, stare, lunge, and bite, unless that's actually what your specific dog does. What behavior does your dog exhibit two behaviors before the bite? And three? Think about how the dog's behaviors flow one into the next and ultimately into that final behavior that is causing the most significant problems. This specific chain of behaviors, no matter what your dog does, is what you're working with, not a list of behaviors in a book or on a website. It's better to learn about your dog's behavior *from your dog.*

Please understand that ethological studies provide useful generalities. You absolutely have to know your species. We know that a lot of dogs will notice, look, stare, freeze, growl, lunge, and bite, but there are some dogs who haven't read the books. They skip certain steps, mix up the order of the steps, and throw in extra steps. It's more important to know your particular dog.

Aggressive behaviors occur in succession, like links in a chain, but they all have a purpose. A dog can't bite you unless he gets close enough, and he can't get close enough if he moves too slowly because you'll get away, so he quickly lunges. Before he lunges, he has to get momentum, so he may back up before lunging. And he won't do any of this before he sees that the "bad guy" is there, so he has to first notice the person or animal. Put all of these steps in motion, and you've got notice, back up, lunge, and bite (again,

not every dog performs the same chain of behaviors). You have to learn what your dog does *before* he behaves aggressively if you want to work safely with your aggressive dog. You've got to know that backing up might be a problem for your dog in a situation in which something he's worried about is approaching. You've also got to be aware of what he does when he notices the other person or dog. You can't text and safely walk your aggressive dog at the same time. You've got to pay attention to your dog.

If you intervene as soon as he performs one of these behaviors by punishing the dog, you may extinguish only one link out of the chain, not the whole chain of behavior, because the dog is still worried

Is staring part of your dog's chain of aggressive behavior?

about the situation and still doesn't know any other way to deal with it. A lot of people punish the warning growl out of their dogs' behavior chains, so they end up with dogs who bite without first conveying clearly that they can't take any more. Growls are our friends. Don't punish them. All of the behaviors in your dog's preaggression chain may become good warning signs if you learn them.

You have to give your dog back some managed control of his world that things like leashes and fences take away from him. The idea is to teach him that there are things he can do that will make the bad guy go away or the bad thing stop happening without behaving aggressively. The more you limit his choices, the more likely he is to behave aggressively. Give him choices and alternatives.

As a pet owner, even if you don't have any training in canine behavior, you have an unusual sort of advantage. You can start thinking logically about your dog's specific behaviors right from the start rather than learning a lot of dog-training folklore first. You may have thought your dog bit someone right out of the blue. You may think that his aggression is just not predictable. But there are other behaviors that happen before the aggressive ones that you can learn to notice. It may be

This dog's preaggression behavior is unmistakable.

that your dog has a short fuse and it all happens so quickly that it's hard to see the succession of behaviors, but there are things that he does in advance.

You can't deny that your dog does a lot of things that other members of his species do, even if he was raised by a cat in a litter of squirrels and never laid eyes on another dog. He's a dog. He does dog things. But a dog raised by a cat will also do cat things, and a dog raised by a cat with a litter of squirrels will also do things that squirrels raised by cats with one dog sibling do. Your dog is now part of your human family, so he's going to do some things because the human world requires it. For example, he won't move away from trouble if he's hooked to you by a leash and you don't let him leave. You have to help him learn that you will support him in making good decisions.

I heard about a newly adopted dog who was hanging out with his new owners, toward whom he had shown a great deal of affection during their short time as a family. He was on the floor as his owners sat on the couch, watching TV. One of the owners reached down to pet the dog, and the dog instantly lunged up. As the owner ducked to avoid the bite, the dog grabbed the woman's scalp with her teeth and held on. The owner ended up with twenty-five staples in the top of her head.

If we were going to work with this dog for aggression, what chain of behaviors would we work with? She definitely noticed. But that's not enough information. *How* did she notice? *What*

did she notice? Dogs notice when someone pets them, and dogs notice when someone swings a bat at them, and dogs notice when there is food in their bowls. Noticing isn't a problem all by itself. But if noticing people results in biting them, we'd better be noticing what our dogs notice.

One approach to working with aggression is to teach the dog to look at his owner instead of whoever he doesn't like. This can be a very useful management tool, but it doesn't teach the dog to deal with whatever they don't like. With this dog, it seems as if she didn't have time to look at her owner for long. The owner petted the dog and instantly was under attack. If the dog froze or stared, it was only briefly. We can't start our observation of this dog with growling or barking. Why? She didn't do those things. She lunged, bit, and held on. She bit hard enough that it was difficult for the other owner to dislodge the dog so they could go to the hospital. Her owners didn't see the behaviors that we expect to lead up to aggression. They probably didn't even have time to think to look for them. In that situation, this dog had a short fuse.

If we were to have worked with this dog, we would have had to start earlier than lunge and bite in her chain of behaviors to prevent her from doing what she did. Just like your dog, this dog is unique and has her own unique history. She did what *she* did, not what many books say she should have done. Sometimes we end up with dogs who seem to bite "out of the blue" because people assume that aggression always involves a big display. Maybe you thought a dog would always growl, bark, or snarl before biting, so you completely missed your dog's subtle attempt to move away, or the extreme way he tried to avoid your hand when you went to pat the top of his head, or how he scratches himself every time you lean over him. Your dog may very well do some of what the books say, and some books are extremely helpful in learning about the canine species in general. But as you set about working with your individual dog, you will see that he has his own set of behaviors. Your observations of your dog are essential. What did your dog do just before he bit? What about just before that? And just before that?

What happened with this dog before she lunged upward and delivered her bite? I suspect, but cannot say for sure, that she was asleep. (To make a fair assessment, I would need to know for sure, and you will need to know for sure when watching your dog, too.) Plus, she had a known history of abuse. Her new owner touched her lovingly during her sleep, and, from her sleepy wilderness, she woke in a still-unfamiliar environment, launched upward toward her presumed attacker, and attacked her back. If I were working with this dog, I would start her treatment by teaching the owners to never touch her while she was asleep. Instead, they would awaken her with a sound or make sure she only slept in a crate. Management has to be part of behavior modification.

The behavior you're going to work with is not the bite. You don't start with the risky behavior because it's too late and too dangerous. You're going to work with the behavior that happens just before, two behaviors before, or, better yet, six, seven, or eight behaviors before the bite. You're going to concentrate on the behaviors that consistently lead up to a bite. You're going to show the dog that he doesn't need to look, stare, growl, lunge, and bite or any combination of preaggressive behaviors to stay safe because you're never going to punish him for doing those things. You're going to give him alternatives.

What CAT will show your dog is that he can just look, turn his head, sit, and tilt his head to the side. Or he can look at the other dog, nudge Mom's hand for a pet, and "look at the other dog" again. The key is to figure out where safe behaviors like look at the other dog end and where the aggressive behaviors like "lunge" and "bite" start. And we want to make sure that safe behaviors pay off so well that your dog understands that he doesn't need aggressive behaviors anymore.

The whole chain of behaviors leading up to aggression can be treated as one big behavior in many cases if you are using a constructional approach to training rather than a punishing approach. If your dog always freezes, stares, backs up, lunges, and then bites, we can start by treating freezing as an undesirable behavior. The behavior of freezing is not dangerous all by itself, but if you observe that freezing is always or usually the first part of the

Backing up and barking are part of this dog's behavior chain.

biting behavior chain, we can start there. Instead of punishing freezing, which, as we discussed, will leave your dog with no knowledge of what to do instead and will just make him start with a link in the chain that is closer to a bite, and therefore make him more dangerous, we will teach him what he can do instead of freezing. You'll set up a training procedure that will give him exactly what he wants and needs to feel safe in his world. Let's teach the dog something other than freezing that is easy to do and effective in getting rid of scary strangers. This will keep the procedure safer for you and anyone you're working with or near, and your dog will likely get the idea that his whole aggressive behavior chain isn't necessary and is way too much work. Let's show him easier things he can do that will result in the peace and security he wants and needs.

Make learning these new behaviors as easy as possible for your dog. The goal is to stop him from feeling that he's under threat of imminent danger, either from the scary thing he normally behaves aggressively toward or from any punishment from you. One of the ways we do this is by starting out with the dog or person toward whom your dog behaves aggressively, or someone who has volunteered to work with you, as far away as possible (we refer to this person or dog as the *helper*). In the CAT procedure, we start working far enough away in terms of physical distance that Fido doesn't feel worried when he looks at the person or other dog. This is very important. While there will be times in the process when you

Turning his head and licking his lips are two examples of alternative behaviors.

It's important to emphasize here that the process is about more than the dog not behaving aggressively. It's also about picking neutral or friendly behaviors that you can reinforce as the safe behaviors that the dog learns to use to replace aggression. If he turns his head, great. If he sits, fabulous. If he walks away, walk away with him.

But what happens if he performs one of the behaviors we want to replace? Freezing, growling, barking, lunging? You will avoid pushing the dog to the point of aggression, but sometimes you'll miss. In this case, as long as all necessary safety procedures and equipment are in place, the helper simply stays put and lets the dog figure out what he can do that will be more effective than this mess of behavior. When barking, growling, and being a maniac don't produce the results he wants, he'll try other things. Your goal is to show the dog, "Hey, aggression isn't going to work now, but you can do any of a vast array of safe, friendly, or neutral behaviors, and that scary person will hit the road fast as you please. Oh, and, Fido? You can try out any behavior you want."

Over time, you will ask your dog to tolerate some variables, such as the helper being a little closer for a longer time, the helper moving around more, working

will miss the mark or your dog will surprise you, the goal is to make it easy for him.

The helper will walk forward just until the dog notices him or her and then will stop. Then, if the dog decides the helper is so far away that it's no big deal and does something that isn't aggressive, the helper will walk away and wait. Every fifteen to sixty seconds, the decoy will walk forward, and if the dog does not behave aggressively, he or she will walk away again.

This sounds counterintuitive, right? Walking away as a reward? But it works. Why does it work? Because what the dog wants most of all is relief. He wants the thing that's worrying him to go away and leave him alone. And that's what this program starts out by doing. We're telling the dog that we understand that this is hard, and we understand that he needs a break. So we have the worrisome person (or animal) walk away.

at different times of day, and working in different locations. But we will make these changes in little bite-sized pieces so the dog can succeed as easily as possible; we don't expect him to figure it out in a gigantic, guaranteed-failure chunk.

When we start again after an unsuccessful attempt when the dog behaved aggressively, we will often make some adjustments before we try again. If he looked at the person and then growled, we're probably pushing too hard and need to back off and work from farther away on the next approach. Or maybe we're expecting him to look calmly at the other dog for ten seconds without starting to growl when he's really ready to do it for only three seconds. In this case, we'll have our helper walk away only two seconds after the dog looks at him or her instead of waiting so long that the dog produces an undesirable behavior. Why wait two seconds when we know he can do three? Because the goal is to make it as easy as possible for your dog to do the right thing.

DID YOU KNOW?

Aggression is stressful for dogs, not just for owners. It's difficult and exhausting for a dog to live on the edge of alarm all the time, and the stress can cause health issues.

Try two seconds when he can probably do three seconds and then work up from there. If you go too far and he aggresses, back off again.

If the dog looks at the helper and then gets up and walks away, that's great. Because we're always paying attention, we see that he has looked at the person or dog without behaving aggressively and chose all by himself to move away from him or her, so we're going to reward that behavior by walking away with him. The key is to show him that he has choices other than aggression and that the alternatives will be even more effective. Leaning on his owner? Great! Walking away from something he used to attack? Wonderful!

When your dog's aggression started, he learned that if he barked, growled, lunged, and bit, people or other dogs went away and left him alone. Good teaching is when you let the learner figure something out within planned limits. Then his response can be, "OK, if I see him but I walk the other way, then everything's cool and I don't have to deal with a fight. My person is cool with it, and everything is good." Obviously, you're going to redirect him from walking into traffic or from walking toward an oncoming dog using the most casual approach possible.

Another important point to note is that if the dog tries to go away from what he usually barks at, and you let him completely leave the situation for good, he's not going to learn much more than that all he has to do is just run away and things will be fine. How does that help

The helper remains far from the dog.

The helper reaches a point where the dog reacts.

When the dog displays calm or neutral behavior, the helper rewards the dog by turning and walking away.

him or you when he is in the proximity of people or animals that worry him? If you live in apartment, he still has to walk in public to go to the bathroom every day. If he has to go to the vet, he's still going to have to be around people and other animals sometimes. You are going to work very hard to make this process as easy for him as possible, but, like every good teacher, you will do your best to break the work down into manageable pieces. You won't benefit him by letting him skip his homework (never addressing the aversive situation at all) or by doing it for him (dragging him away).

Did I say that you would never drag your dog away when he starts to behave aggressively? There is one exception. When things go wrong, sometimes you have to cut your losses. If that other dog slips his leash, or if a teenager runs toward your dog, squealing and ready to hug, you just yell an order: "Get your dog!" or "Stop! Don't touch my dog!" and you skedaddle. Yep, it can feel rude to say that to the nice, excited kid, but isn't it better than the teen wearing a facial scar to her prom and your dog spending ten days in quarantine at animal control?

Cutting your losses isn't ideal. It can set you back a bit in your training, but the truth is that sometimes that's your best bet. Save your dog from the off-leash dog, save the teenager from a bite, go home and think about your game plan some more. Think about every walk with your dog as a training session. Think about not going for walks at all for the time being and exercising him in your backyard if you have one. Or walk your dog late at night or early in the morning if you can do so safely until you've done enough work to try working when there are only a few people out.

Pay attention to what else is going on when your dog exhibits the problem behavior. You can change many behaviors by changing something about the environment. Does it usually happen when he is eating? Does it happen mostly around his toys? Is he protecting his favorite place? Maybe it has to do with being startled. Does it happen when someone surprises him, like a person suddenly showing up behind him? In this case, teaching people not to sneak up on your dog would be a great idea. Could it be that he is experiencing some sort of pain? Have you had that checkup with the vet? Is he hungry? Sometimes splitting the daily ration between a morning and evening meal instead of one meal a day and giving a treat-stuffed chew toy in the middle of the day can make a big difference in behavior. We discovered years ago at the first shelter I worked at that when dogs are fed twice a day, they are easier to handle than when they are fed once a day. Does he have his own place where he can be left alone when the kids are being rowdy? Is there anything else about the environment that you can change to improve your dog's behavior?

DID YOU KNOW?

The kind of lesson that a dog learns through harsh treatment is likely to backfire. I understand that it may seem as if the dog needs to "learn his lesson," but let's show your dog that the world isn't as dangerous as he thought so that he can make better choices.

We also discovered at the shelter that cold dogs don't behave well in a variety of ways. They jump around, are noisy, and may be irritable, which increases the risk of bites or accidental injuries. We discovered this when the central heating went out one winter in one of the shelters. Some dogs huddled pitifully in their beds while others ran and jumped incessantly. (Needless to say, we had it fixed as quickly as possible and used space heaters until the repairs were made.)

Toward whom does your dog behave aggressively? Aggression is situation-specific, and the things dogs are aggressive toward are specific for them, too. A dog may be completely friendly toward one person but severely aggressive toward another. A dog may be friendly toward a person in one situation and unfriendly toward that same person in another situation. A dog may initially exhibit

DO NOT DRAG

There's something very important to note here. If the dog makes the choice to walk away, that is awesome, cool, groovy, the bee's knees, simply grand! But you should never pull the dog away to make him do something nonaggressive unless it's to protect someone from being hurt. Pulling the dog away is not teaching; it's just dragging. Your dog will not learn that turning and walking away solved the problem. He will learn, "When that scary thing is around, my owner freaks out and chokes me, and we run away." There is learning in that, but it's not the learning you want.

problematic behaviors toward strangers but gradually warm up to them. He may like some dogs and not others. He may love people and hate dogs. He may love adults but not children. And sometimes it's quite hard to figure out exactly what triggers the aggressive behavior because it can be ridiculously specific.

I once worked with a family whose Bull Terrier, Blanca, was great with everyone except for the wife's sister, Sara. Sara visited often, and the dog had bitten her multiple times. On a few occasions, the dog had pinned her in a bedroom, where she had to stay until the husband could come home from work to call the dog off. He couldn't believe it. Blanca was a perfect lady when he was at home, and he thought they were being ridiculous to call him home from work because of the dog.

As we were sleuthing out just what was going on, the wife and Sara said it only happened when the husband was at work. This is what I observed as well. Blanca was great with Sara when I met the three of them together. Then I asked the husband to wait in a different room. The dog still acted friendly toward Sara. He went into the garage. No change. He went into the backyard. Nothing. He got in the car and drove away. *Bingo*! The dog snarled and charged at Sara. Blanca was only aggressive when the husband drove away from the house in his car. What a challenge! But once we knew that, we were able to make progress with Blanca by working with the wife and sister when the husband was not at home. That husband said that until he saw my video of his dog lunging at his sister-in-law, he had trouble believing that it actually happened. Blanca simply didn't act that way around him. So you're not crazy if you think your dog seems to have very specific aggression.

Think about the time of day, whether the dog is hungry, and whether there's a lot of activity or noise happening, such as when the family gets home in the evening, when guests are over, or when workers are in the house. Work on pinpointing the specific conditions under which your dog behaves aggressively and set up ways to make those occasions easier on the dog.

Dragging your dog away is a last resort, only to be used to prevent injury or damage.

The word *constructional* is important. As I've mentioned, this is the key concept in the CAT procedure. *Construct* means "build." Our goal is to build desirable behaviors that will take the place of problem behaviors. Most methods of working to resolve aggression focus on getting rid of problem behaviors. We are going to focus on building very strong desirable behaviors using behaviors that are already in the dog's repertoire as a foundation. We're going to teach desirable behaviors that the dog can do instead of aggressive behaviors that are just as effective—or even more effective—than the problem behaviors in achieving an outcome that is valuable to the dog (namely, getting people and dogs he doesn't like to go away). We're going to teach the dog that easier behaviors can get the same results.

You will let your dog learn as many alternative behaviors as possible. While I was doing the CAT research with Dr. Rosales, I worked with a Greyhound named Trixie. Like Blanca, Trixie had very specific aggressive behavior. With Trixie, the aggression happened only in the living room of the home. Unlike Blanca's aggression toward a specific person and only when the husband was gone, Trixie aggressed toward all visitors, but we were to learn that it was mostly in the presence of the male owner, whom she loved.

Trixie was one of the first few dogs I worked with, and I set about actively reinforcing a behavior she offered often: turning her head away from me. At first, she would bark while staring at me. As soon as she turned her head, I walked away. I made that behavior very strong by walking away every time she did it.

A dog may act aggressively only in a certain place, such as his favorite spot on the couch.

The next thing you know, old Trixie was turning her head to the side and barking at me with her eyes turned as far to the front as she could make them go so that she could see me. Call it a rookie mistake, but strange things can come up in aggression work, so don't be surprised. Behavior works in orderly ways, but sometimes it's hard to figure out the order.

Dr. Rosales and I looked at my videos of Trixie several times. His recommendation was to stop walking away when she turned her head. Instead, he said, turn away when she does anything that isn't aggression. Turning her head. Sitting. Scratching her neck. Leaning on her owner.

Another time, Dr. Rosales and I were in Canada, conducting a CAT seminar. On the second day of the seminar, we did a live demo with a few different aggressive dogs. One of the dogs, a Smooth Collie, had been labeled aggressive a couple of years earlier. The owner had diligently tried technique after technique to help her dog. What we found was a dog who did nothing when she saw us. She did nothing as we worked closer and closer to her. But something wasn't right. Sure enough, once I got close enough that the dog thought she could reach me, she went from doing nothing to launching at me with a roar in a second flat. What this dog had learned in all her aggression training was to lay low until the bad guy (ahem, me) was close enough to increase her odds of contact. That was certainly not what we wanted to accomplish.

In aggression work, the word *calm* is used often. You want to help your dog feel calm in the face of his adversary, so to speak. But *calm* is not the same thing as *still*. It's easy to assume that if a dog is just lying there, he's feeling relaxed. Not necessarily. He might just have learned that the less movement he makes, the fewer problems he has, and that if the creepy person does get close enough, being still will give him a chance to strike.

Yes, we want the dog to feel confident and not to worry that his world is unsafe. But instead of teaching the dog to show us less behavior, it's so much easier to work with a dog who shows us a lot of behavior so we know what we're working with. I would much rather work with a roaring lion of a dog than a dog that is quiet and doesn't move. Some of the scariest dogs I've ever known were very still.

The next time I faced a still dog, I didn't mistake him for a calm dog. I knew he could very well be a dog that had learned to be still—in other words, motionless—because it was effective. If the dog in front of you has already learned to be very still, you'll have to walk away when

he makes any small movement, such as twitching his eyebrow, or adjusting his weight slightly, or exhaling audibly, and gradually work up to the dog's moving around and doing things that we can more easily reinforce. This is very tedious work, but it can be done. The best bet is to reinforce movement throughout the process.

When the dog moves more, you can select gradually safer and friendlier behaviors. For example, let's say I'm working as the helper with a dog. The dog stands and looks at me, which is what he's been doing the last three times I approached him, but then he turns his side to me. I can pick that side turn as the behavior I want to strengthen. Because I walk away when he turns, and we've established that he is

Look for a variety of visible behaviors, such as a head turn, to reward.

doing things that he knows will make me walk away, he's going to turn away more often when I approach in the future. And I'll keep walking away when he turns, as well as when he walks, sits, tilts his head, or snaps at a fly. And he'll begin to choose those behaviors over lying perfectly still or instead of barking and growling as he might have been doing previously.

We're going to teach as many safe, desirable alternatives as we can by having the "bad guy" walk away when the dog does any of his range of nonaggressive behaviors; the more, the better. This way, Fido doesn't learn that sitting still and looking at his owner is the only way to deal with problems. He also doesn't learn that waiting motionlessly until the stranger is in proximity before behaving aggressively is an effective tool. He learns that sitting and looking at Mom, or walking away, or rolling over, or playing with a toy, or any number of other safe behaviors can be ways to deal with problems.

We also won't be teaching your dog that treats are the key to avoiding problems. Let me be very clear. Treats are very, very, *very* good training tools, even with aggression work. But right now we have to think about why the dog behaves aggressively in the first place. Does he try to bite your favorite uncle because your uncle gives him treats? Unlikely. He probably bites Uncle Matt because he wants him to go away or stop whatever the heck else he's doing. How valuable is a piece of cheese right then? Fido might eat it. Or he might not. But the treat isn't what the dog wants most in the world at that moment. Why not use the most powerful reward possible—the reward the dog has already told you with his behavior that he wants more than anything else in this specific situation—as the training reward for doing things other than behaving aggressively[5]?

Using treats as your primary aggression-training reward is basically telling Fido that something unrelated to his real-life problem is going to have to be good enough. Fido's not buying it. If it's not good enough, it's simply not good enough. We want Fido to figure out that the world is not such a terrible place, and that if he acts nicely, he's going to get exactly what he has been trying to tell us he wants. He's going to get Uncle Matt to go away. And once he figures out that Matt will go away when he looks at Mom or sits or rolls over or lies on his mat, he's going to do these desirable behaviors much more often in the future.

There are great uses for treats in the training process for aggression. You will use treats to train a variety of skills that will help in the CAT process, like wearing a muzzle, lying on a mat, and turning away when you don't want him to see someone coming from the other direction. But you're going to train all of these behaviors as fun games, when there is no bad guy in the vicinity. You're not going to try to train these behaviors when things are serious, when your dog only knows

---

5 The technical term is *functional reinforcer.*

how to aggress to make the "baddies" get out of town.

So, here's a big part of the treatment. Pay attention.

Instead of giving Fido a treat when he does something we like, we're going to take away something scary when he does something right. The reason is that we want to use the most powerful reinforcer in the world for this individual dog in this situation. Is the dog aggressive to get treats? Unlikely. He's aggressive to create conditions in which he feels safer. So we're going to help him feel safe. We're going to ask Uncle Matt to move away whenever Fido does something good or whenever you tell him it's time. And Fido is going to do those good things more often because they produce really good results for him.

The comment that often comes up at this point is, "But, I don't want to have to make my favorite uncle leave every time my dog is nice to him." And this is the good news. It was most unexpected to me in our research, although Dr. Rosales had seen it before. It was a very nice surprise. As you do the work, and you're getting nicer and nicer behaviors from the dog, the dog will get curious. He'll start to offer curious behaviors, like sniffing the air toward Uncle Matt or maybe a little low tail wag or maybe even keeping his body soft when Uncle Matt approaches. You're making some serious progress by this time. You keep having Uncle Matt walk away, but eventually you'll be sure that the dog wants to check out this uncle. You'll let Fido get close enough to sniff the air, but not touch, because we don't want to flirt with the devil. Next, maybe you take a walk with Uncle Matt beside you, a few feet away. Or have Uncle Matt walk in front of you and Fido so Fido can look really closely at him and check him out without being worried about Matt looking at him. And then you'll practice with Uncle Matt walking behind you and Fido so Fido can get used to having people behind him where he can't get a good look at them the whole time. If he wants to stop and turn around and look, that's fine. Tell Uncle Matt to chill for a minute, and let Fido take a look. Then start walking again.

At this point, something pretty cool can happen. Fido might start to like Uncle Matt. He may start to see that Uncle Matt gets it. Uncle Matt doesn't try any funny business. Continue to have Uncle Matt walk away when Fido does good stuff. After all, that's what got you this far. But if Fido wants to approach Uncle Matt, and his body is soft and fluid, then maybe let them briefly meet. Now, Uncle Matt may want to ruffle Fido's ruff, but don't allow that yet. Just a little bit at a time. A short sniff of Uncle Matt's jeans, and then everyone casually walks away from each other again.

Many times, a lot of dogs decide that Uncle Matt doesn't need to go away anymore. And that's just great. You'll continue to keep their interactions short, though. Next, you'll start having Uncle Matt play a little "hard to get" and leave Fido wanting more.

2

CHANGE IS IN YOUR HANDS: BE PROACTIVE

It doesn't necessarily matter whether you have years of experience handling many different dogs or this is your first and only pet. What matters is your willingness to start where you are and learn. There are many people who have worked in shelters, kennels, and veterinary clinics and those who may be dog trainers themselves who do not have the right skill set to work with aggressive dogs despite many years of handling dogs. There are others who, despite having very little handling experience with dogs, have a natural sense of how to observe dogs and how to convince them to behave differently. If this second type of person also educates him- or herself extensively on the behavior and training of dogs by reading, attending seminars and workshops, and getting plenty of hands-on time with dogs, he or she can do it. Does that sound like you? I know many people who became dog trainers not just because they loved dogs but because they loved one particular aggressive dog and were dedicated to helping that dog. Many, many of those people were not dog professionals when that one dog came into their lives—the dog led them to their niche, they recognized the need, and they stuck with it.

One of the big challenges with working with aggressive dogs is that it's hard to find people who know what they're doing. If you search online, you're going to find a lot of websites for people claiming they are dog-aggression experts. But when you try to figure out how such a trainer goes about his or her work, you'll see that the website doesn't really describe what techniques the trainer uses. You can often identify red flags; for example, a trainer who advertises guaranteed results that can happen in a few hours for several hundred dollars. Or a trainer who offers to board your dog for a couple of weeks and train him. Some board-and-trains are excellent, but some use shock collars and other punishments, so when your dog comes home, he's either "calm" in the sense we talked about earlier (in truth, he's shut down) or he's worse in some way. If you're not allowed to see your dog while he's in board-and-train, not even by remote video, be concerned that there's something the trainer doesn't want you to see, such as your dear dog friend being mistreated during his "vacation." It happens. Using a shock collar on a dog who is completely overwhelmed is not humane, and it won't help the dog learn how to behave in more desirable ways.

Another red flag is a trainer who claims to use treats to train, but then says that no two dogs can be trained the same way. This is a subterfuge, meaning that trainer does some training with treats and some with punishment or corrections. It's called *balanced training* and can result in what is known as the *poisoned cue*. The poisoned cue refers to a behavior that has been trained by using both positive reinforcement and forceful coercion. The dog gets confused and doesn't know whether his efforts are going to help him gain a treat or avoid punishment, so he exhibits stress signals and is unsure about how to correctly respond to commands or cues. His behavior is conflicted because he never knows if

he will be rewarded or punished when he hears a signal to perform a behavior.

Karen Pryor first recognized the poisoned cue phenomenon in her work with marine animals, and then Dr. Rosales and a student named Nicole Murray looked more closely into it at the University of North Texas. Balanced/poisoned-cue training is not good training, and I don't recommend it. I want dogs to be confident in performing alternative behaviors to aggression.

Many excellent trainers don't work with aggressive dogs. Such a trainer may suggest that you locate a veterinary behaviorist, which is great if one is available to you. There are approximately sixty Diplomates of the American College of Veterinary Behaviorists, and a few of them are in the United Kingdom. The challenge here is obvious. There may not be a veterinary behaviorist anywhere near you; if there is one, he or she is likely to be very busy. Some behaviorists don't work exclusively in behavior, and some do not see private clients. If you're advised to work with a veterinary behaviorist, ask your trainer for a referral.

Sometimes you're the only resource you've got. You've already been handling your dog, but you're the one who has to answer the question of whether you can train your dog safely and well. In this chapter, I'm going to ask you some challenging questions. I recommend reading this chapter with a partner who also loves your dog so that you can bounce things off each other and get a good feel for what is really possible. This partner should be someone you can truly trust and truly be open and honest with.

If you really love your dog, if you care about what happens to the people or animals toward whom he behaves aggressively, and if you want the best possible outcome, it is essential that you answer my questions honestly. If you begin to suspect or know that you simply won't or can't do the work, you've got some soul searching to do. This dog is going to need your support even when he's not acting very likable, and you're going to need to be committed (to the dog, not to an institution.)

I understand how hard it is to be frank when it comes to your dog's problem behaviors. Good grief—we love our dogs, don't we? Besides, your dog isn't aggressive toward *you*, is he? At least not all the time. So read this chapter with your heart wide open and tell yourself the truth about every question you encounter while reading it. Read this chapter repeatedly if you need to. Read it slowly and let the questions simmer before you decide what your next step will be.

Is everyone in your family up for this?

Often, a dog's aggressive behavior is something that some family members want to work through while others are opposed, afraid, or just not up for it for any of a variety of reasons. Maybe the dog is aggressive toward a person who doesn't want to deal with it. It's no fun to be the one who has to be on high alert all the time. This person may believe that a child or someone else in the family, possibly another pet, is at risk. The opposite can sometimes be true, too. Sometimes the parents don't want to break the children's hearts by giving up the dog. Every responsible adult in the household has to be on board for the best outcome. The children's needs must be taken into account, but ultimately it's up to the grown-ups to make the decision.

Depending on the severity of the aggression and how manageable the dog is, it might be possible for someone in the family to be hands-off with the dog instead of participating in training, but that will put a big responsibility on others in the family: the responsibility to be 100 percent consistent. Trainers often say, "Management always fails." We've discussed that management means

implementing tools and practices that prevent problems, like putting a muzzle on the dog, crating the dog when guests come over, or, in some cases, sedating the dog to go to the vet. It doesn't mean you shouldn't bother with management—you definitely must. It means that sooner or later someone is going to leave the gate open or forget that the dog is loose when he or she answers the door. Keep reading, and I'll help you determine if your management plan is workable before you make up your mind.

Has your dog ever bitten anyone? How bad was the bite?

If your dog has already bitten, you know why I'm asking these questions. But even if your dog has not bitten yet, thinking about these questions will help you get a handle on how badly the dog may potentially hurt someone. Ian Dunbar, DVM, created a bite-assessment scale that rates the intensity of a bite on a scale of 1 to 6. The way we actively treat the aggressive response is similar in all dogs, whether a Level 1 or a Level 6 biter, but the safety precautions you need to take during training and between training sessions may be dramatically different based on the bite level. More severe bites put additional very serious considerations on the table. The size and power of your dog are important considerations, too.

There are six levels on Dr. Dunbar's scale; following is a paraphrased version with my comments.

LEVEL 1

Dog growls, lunges, snaps, or snarls, but teeth do not touch the skin.

LEVEL 2

Teeth touch skin, but there is no puncture. There may be red marks or minor bruises from the dog's muzzle or teeth.

According to Dr. Dunbar, Levels 1 and 2 comprise more than 99 percent of incidents related to dog bites or attempted bites. The dog is not dangerous yet and may be more likely to be successful in a behavior-modification protocol. As long as he hasn't produced higher level bites in addition to these minor bites, either at the same time or at a separate time, you may be able to safely work with him. The dog needs basic training for manners, cooperation, and self-control, and you should manage him by using a crate appropriately, keeping him behind closed doors when people or dogs toward whom he may behave aggressively are around, and using leashes and other tools to prevent him from ever having the opportunity to bite. Start obedience training immediately, and start CAT as soon as you learn it. Before the dog discovers on his own that more intense bites work even better than soft bites, we want to make sure he learns that there are ways to deal with a problem other than behaving aggressively.

The goal for training with CAT is that we are going to teach this dog a lot of safe, friendly ways to behave, and we

Left: Does your dog end his chain of aggressive behaviors with a bite?

Below: When used properly, a crate can be a valuable management tool.

are also going to teach him that you will never put him in situations he can't handle. You're going to be his advocate. If he doesn't want strangers to touch him, strangers don't get to touch him. If your Aunt Mimi likes to scoop him up because he looks just like a dog she used to have, and she will not comply with your instructions, you will crate him in a separate room whenever Aunt Mimi comes over. Your house, your dog, your rules. If a neighborhood child throws things at him when he's out in the backyard, he will never again be outside in the backyard alone, and you will contact the parents of this child to let them know what has happened. (I love kids, but I think we do them a great disservice by allowing them to mistreat animals. Animals are likely to go on the defensive, and the child is likely to get hurt.)

As part of the treatment, you have to determine not to expose your dog to new situations in which he can strengthen his knowledge that aggression works to get him what he wants: distance from things he doesn't like. Don't let him learn new conditions under which aggression works for him. Keep him home. Exercise him in your enclosed backyard or walk him late at night and early in the morning when

not many people are out walking their dogs. We hope that we can work past this with Level 1 and 2 dogs, but not in the first stages of training.

LEVEL 3

The bite has left puncture wounds approximately half the length of one of the dog's canine teeth. There are one to four punctures, but all resulted from only a single bite. No tearing or slashes. The victim was not shaken from side to side. There may be bruising.

The potential for successful work with a Level 3 biter, according to Dr. Dunbar, is fair to good. In my view, this is true, as long as the trainer is able to handle the dog safely and is very consistent about maintaining training and management. However, behavior modification can be time-consuming and is not risk-free. This

dog may bite again, and his bites may become more severe over time, especially if he gets a chance to learn that softer bites no longer work. The same rules for managing others around your dog and preventing your dog from learning new situations in which to behave aggressively apply for a Level 3.

LEVEL 4

There are one to four puncture wounds from a single bite; one hole is deeper than half the length of a canine tooth, and usually there was contact from other teeth in addition to the canine teeth. There may be significant bruising, tears, and/or slashing wounds. The dog clamped down and shook the victim.

Level 4 bites come from dogs that are very dangerous. You should work with a Level 4 dog only under the direct supervision of an experienced trainer or behaviorist who understands the science of behavior and will not slap a shock collar on him. This dog's behavior can be changed—all behavior can change—but the outlook for treatment is not good because it will be dangerous to work with a hard-biting dog. It's just plain difficult to manage this kind of situation safely. We can definitely do things that will help this dog improve, but will he ever forget how to bite? No. There is a chance it could happen again if the conditions support biting.

I think most Level 4, 5, and 6 dogs should be under protected contact, a procedure used in zoos to protect keepers from injuries by dangerous animals.

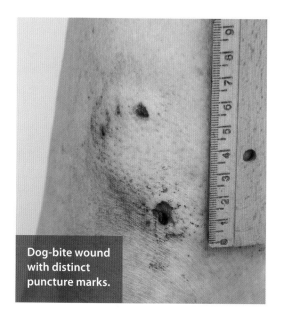

Dog-bite wound with distinct puncture marks.

LEVEL 5

Multiple-bite incident with at least two Level 4 bites or multiple attack incidents with at least one Level 4 bite in each.

My advice is that you do not try to work with this dog. If you do, it must be under the close supervision of a very skilled trainer or behaviorist experienced in treating canine aggression without the use of force and pain. If you use force and pain to train this dog, he is very likely to become more dangerous.

LEVEL 6

Any bite resulting in death of a human.

This dog is simply too dangerous to live with people. To keep this dog, he would need to remain in solitary confinement, and that is no life for a dog. Dr. Dunbar recommends euthanasia because the quality of life is so poor for dogs who have to live out their lives this way, and I completely agree. Dogs do not understand the concept of end-of-life; they only know right now. They know when they are bored, scared, defensive, and so forth. Their lives will be all about knowing misery if they are kept alive after a Level 6 bite. No matter how much we love an aggressive dog, we owe him an exit from confinement and the insanity that invariably comes along with it.

People have been killed accidentally by elephants and other exotic animals, and people have been killed on purpose because something went wrong and the animals got angry. The same is true for dogs. Taking on the responsibility to train a dog with this bite history is an enormous responsibility. If you suspect or observe that any person who will be around this dog will not follow your safety instructions, or if you will hesitate for any reason to firmly deliver safety instructions, you will not be able to safely work with this dog.

Also consider how the dog's life will be. He will have to be locked in a crate a lot of the time. He will not be able to go out on walks. His quality of life will be at least changed, if not drastically diminished. Mistakes, such as forgetting to lock the gate or failing to notice a break in the fence, can be innocent mistakes that have tragic outcomes.

There are three things to consider:

1. Can the dog be managed safely during behavior modification?
2. What will the dog's quality of life be during and after behavior modification (if behavior modification ever ends)?

Will a Level 6 dog's life in a kennel be a life worth living? I've seen a lot of dogs develop what can only be called *kennel insanity* because confinement is too hard for them to endure.

3. What is the likelihood of effective rehabilitation? Can we improve his behavior? Can we improve it to the point where we can guarantee he'll never bite anyone ever again, ever? There are too many variables to know for sure.

I understand that families love dogs who have bitten them badly, even owners whose dogs have bitten *them* badly. It's still a matter of protecting people and other animals from this dog. If the dog has bitten other animals, sometimes a change of environment will work; for example, giving a chicken-killing dog to a family in a community where there are no chickens or ensuring that a dog has no access to small dogs or cats may work. The latter gets more complicated because how do you know when a cat will dart out from the bushes and cross your path or when a person walking a small dog will appear on your street?

Rabies quarantine laws are another consideration. In most communities in the United States, laws require animals who bite and draw blood be quarantined for, usually, ten days. Some communities will allow in-home quarantines for

first offenses, but others will require that the animal be quarantined in an animal control facility for the duration. Laws vary about whether you can get your pet back after quarantine, and the situation surrounding the bite will play into decisions also. If the injury your dog caused was significant, it may be up to a judge. In the worst case, your dog may be deemed a dangerous dog and be euthanized.

I know that was hard to read, but it only takes a quick Internet search to learn why many professionals support these laws. You can easily find photographs of what has happened to people of all ages when they were bitten by dogs, and they are not easy to look at. There are also news stories from around the world of trusted family or resident dogs who killed someone, usually someone in their families. (A *family dog* is a pet who lives his life largely with his family and goes into and out of the house. A *resident dog* is one who lives outside and is not allowed into the house very often, if at all, and spends little social time with the family. Resident dogs tend to have territorial rather than familial relationships with the people in their families and can be more dangerous to their owners as well as to people they consider threats, such as delivery people entering their property.)

While you can perform treatment and be successful to some degree with Level 5 and 6 dogs, if the dog is already biting this severely, he might bite again when a troubling situation arises. When a

situation arises in which the dog's new skills don't work, such as the approach of a stranger who hasn't been coached in CAT, the dog may decide he better go back to his old ways.

I believe that some dogs can only be kept safely in a protected contact setting, but who is going to go to a dog zoo and pay to see them so that the entrance fees can pay for their care? There are friendly dogs everywhere that people can see and play with for free. Dog sanctuaries exist, and some are successful in their own ways, but many of the dogs must remain in solitary confinement forever. It's heartbreaking. Some dog sanctuaries, even some that are legal nonprofit organizations, sometimes end up with so many dogs that they are unable to provide appropriate care, and the animals end up being seized by law enforcement. Yes, really. The best of the best no-kill shelters and pet sanctuaries have limits to how many animals they can take in. When they're full, they have to say no at the door. There's only so much room at the inn. They don't have room for very many dangerous dogs. If this dog enters a sanctuary, what will his long-term quality of life be? Who will love him? Will he have interesting things to do each day? Will he be able to have social interactions, or will he need to be completely isolated for the safety of the staff and other animals? Will he be spending years, even a decade or more, alone in that kennel? The dogs I've seen who have spent many years in such places live very depleted lives despite the efforts of the staff, who do their best. These dogs don't get to be dogs. They are inmates.

Is there a farm where a dangerous dog can go live out his days?

No. I'm sorry. Farmers don't like to be bitten by dogs, either.

Is euthanasia really the worst thing that can happen to a dog with severe or otherwise untreatable aggression?

Forgive me for being blunt, but sometimes, my friends, there are things worse than death. And for dogs with aggression, those things can be lifelong isolation and loneliness; repeated periods of rabies quarantine, boredom, anxiety, physical discomfort, or retaliatory aggression from humans and other animals; and the inability to perform species- and breed-appropriate behaviors, such as running and sniffing new scents, because they're imprisoned. All of these can be excruciating and devastating for living creatures. In some cases of canine aggression, euthanasia is the humane, compassionate choice.

What does saving a dog who has severely injured or killed someone do to the people he has injured, the family and friends of those he has killed? If you're dealing with a dog that has had Level 4, 5, and 6 bites, you absolutely must think some hard thoughts. Some Level 4 dogs can be saved through very hard, very skilled work. Level 5 and 6 dogs are not safe outside isolated confinement.

Can you safely handle your dog?

When your dog lunges toward someone on leash, do you feel like you're going to lose control of him? Have you already lost control of him on one or more occasions? How much does your dog weigh? If you weigh 110 pounds, and your aggressive dog is a 110-pound Great Dane, can you prevent him from attacking someone on a walk if he is determined to attack? Do you have any physical limitations that will keep you from controlling your dog?

All behavior is situation-specific. When you go to a gym to watch a basketball game, you may yell and cheer. When you

A territorial dog may see a well-meaning delivery person as a threat to his property.

A basket muzzle can be helpful when training a dog with a bite history.

go to church, will you behave in the same way? This is how aggression works, too. Blanca, who I previously mentioned, was extremely specific with her aggression. *Only attack the sister, and only when Dad has driven away in the car.* It's not always that specific, but the environment always affects whether the aggressive behavior will happen or not, so you have to train in situations that are similar to the situation in which the aggression occurs. You can't choose a training site because it's convenient unless you can make it similar to the place where the aggression occurs. It's important to consider the conditions under which your dog behaves aggressively as you plan to set up a training environment and as you determine if you are able to set up an appropriate training environment.

For dogs who behave aggressively only on leash, you have to work with the dog on leash. Obviously, you're going to have

to figure out how you can secure him so that he absolutely cannot get access to someone he could hurt during the training. Can you hold your dog safely even if you accidentally go over threshold during training and he lunges? If not, you'll have to figure out an alternative. I once worked with a strong, enormous, ten-month-old English Mastiff who had broken every kind of tether his owners had tried with him until they tried a heavy-duty chain intended for towing trucks. Industrial nylon straps were just chew toys for this 120-pound dog. A tow chain is not an ideal training tether, but, in this case, it was what we had to use for safety. On many occasions with many dogs, I've had clients tether their dogs using two leashes in case one broke. Sometimes owners can manage the leash in their hands, but often we have to find a sturdy post or tree to ensure that the dog could not get loose.

Is your dog aggressive when behind a fence?

Trainers often call this *barrier guarding* or *territorial aggression*. Is the fence secure enough that your dog cannot break through it, and is it tall enough that he cannot jump over it? Can he dig under it? Take the time to ensure that the fence is secure before you start training in a fenced area. In some cases, you may need to start out with a fence and a leash or tether and gradually work toward having the dog loose on one side of the fence.

Is your dog aggressive around children?

Aggression toward children is an extremely dangerous situation. Children are absolutely the most vulnerable when it comes to aggressive dogs, and elderly people come next. If your dog is aggressive toward children, children are

It's rare that a dog actually enjoys hugging. Instead, teach a child to let the dog approach, sit beside the dog, pet the dog with one hand, and keep his or her face away from the dog's.

placed at risk every time he is around them. Conversely, having a dog behave aggressively toward a child could create serious fear issues for the child, and that's just nowhere near acceptable. Finally, how are you going to set up a training environment with a child as the helper? Who on Earth would let their child participate in training an aggressive dog? In some areas, there are trainers who work specifically with families with little kids primarily on management techniques, but it's up to you to consider your dog's bite level and your family's well-being.

One excellent resource is Family Paws Parent Education. This organization licenses trainers around the world, and you can check their website (www. familypaws.com) to see if there is a Family Paws Educator near you. Family Paws founder Jennifer Shryock will also conduct phone consultations. A skilled aggression trainer or your vet may be very helpful resources as you work through these challenges and make difficult decisions.

Consider how calm and patient children always are. *What*? Of course they're not. Children are impulsive. They are fidgety. They may not understand instructions. They fall down. They make noise. They may get bored and not pay attention. This can even be the case with adults as well. Treating aggression is not a game, and treating aggression with children just may not be safe enough to try. It's not only large dogs that can harm children. Brace yourself. Dachshunds and Pomeranians have killed children. Little bites can be lethal.

If your dog is aggressive toward children, you need the help of a trainer who knows how to safely work with aggression cases without using punitive techniques. Work with a trainer or behaviorist to help you set up a safe environment for your child or visiting children.

3

CORRECTIONS AND COERCION IN THE TREATMENT OF AGGRESSION

> In general, all we learn from the inevitable aversives in everyday life is to avoid them if we can.
>
> ~ **Karen Pryor**

Dog owners often feel that their dog must be punished to get rid of his aggressive behavior. Unfortunately, even after punishing the dog, even when it was done under the instruction of a trainer, these dog owners end up calling someone like me because their dog still behaves aggressively. When I worked with aggressive dogs in private practice, I often got calls from people whose dogs weren't any better, or who were worse,

after such training. On the other end of the technique spectrum are trainers who refuse to use anything but treats and kindness to work with aggressive dogs, no matter what the dogs did. Pet owners often don't understand why these trainers don't want the dogs to experience any stress at all.

I understand both sides.

It's true that a lot of "positive" trainers don't use punishments like shock collars or other painful techniques. They are right that corrections can be harsh, and some of us don't have the stomach for it. But there's a reason we don't have a stomach for it, and it's not because we're too soft for this work. I also don't have the stomach for what some dogs do during aggressive episodes. The injuries inflicted on people by aggressive dogs is sometimes extreme. It's perfectly understandable that someone in a fit of fury might lash out at a dog in a punishing way in response to aggression. It's understandable, but it's not helpful. Losing your temper, no matter how understandable it is, probably won't solve the problem. It may make it worse.

As suggested in the epigraph at the beginning of this chapter, aversives occur in everyday life, but they only serve the purpose of teaching us to avoid things that are aversive. If we hurt a dog for attacking someone, what is he going to avoid? He's going to try to avoid being hurt again in whatever way works best to achieve that outcome. Is he going to avoid punishment by simply never behaving aggressively again? I wish it were that simple.

A prong collar is not part of CAT or any other "positive" training method.

Corrections (punishments) work by causing certain behaviors to decrease in certain contexts. What they don't do is build desirable behaviors to replace the aggression. A dog may respond to corrections by not behaving aggressively in the presence of his owner anymore, but instead he may only behave aggressively when left for grooming. Or he may respond by attacking anyone who gets in the way, something trainers refer to as *redirected aggression*. Or he may start chewing holes in the skin of his leg. Seriously. The dog may start hurting himself when he can no longer control his world with his aggression and he isn't given more useful tools to use. He may exhibit a wide variety of behaviors that are just as bad or worse than the original problem. Our goal with CAT is to build desirable behaviors that the dog is more likely to perform than aggressive behaviors.

We don't want to create an animal who lashes out at strangers or his owner or who injures himself. We want an animal who knows a range of alternatives to aggression that will solve his problem safely. Our training should always focus on giving the dog more acceptable tools for dealing with problems he encounters.

If the problems with punishment were just about not wanting to be mean, but I knew that being mean for a moment would resolve a serious aggression problem quickly and effectively, it wouldn't be such a big deal to quickly correct an unpleasant behavior and move on. I would do it myself if it were that simple. However, being mean can backfire.

Make no mistake. I am not teaching people to punish their dogs. While I urge you to learn how punishment works, I very strongly caution you against using punishment or corrections as training or rehabilitation tools. I am discussing it here in some depth because punishment is what people tend to defer to when they're faced with a badly behaving dog. But there are too many risks, both subtle and bold, for you, your dog, members of your family, and your community that can come along with the use of punishment.

Using a prong collar to "correct" your dog's behavior may have the opposite effect.

If you're reading this book to learn about how to reduce your dog's aggression, please understand that using punishment to treat aggression often makes the aggression worse in various ways.

I consider it my responsibility to talk openly about punishment because it is the most natural, knee-jerk, ready-at-a-moment's-notice response to aggression we have at our disposal, and people use it as a behavior-change tool for aggression more often than any other tool. When our dog does something we don't like, such as lunging at Grandma or biting the mail carrier, it's a very common human reaction to just spank him. It's embarrassing and scary when your dog behaves like that, and you just want it to end. So you react like the animal you are, putting your brains aside for the time being, and you punish. This is not a moral failing. It's just not a skillful way to deal with the problem. In order for you

to behave skillfully, we'll need to build a strong nonpunitive repertoire for you. Just like your dog, you need a tool kit of preferred things you can do—things that will work better and that will be safer.

Most people define *punishment* as something we do to a misbehaving person or animal to make him or her stop whatever he or she is doing; with dogs, examples include scolding, spanking with a hand or rolled-up newspaper, or zapping with a shock collar. The reason we almost automatically use punitive measures is that they almost always work to interrupt the behavior in the moment, at least when the behavior is new. Many of us have never learned any other behavior-change tools for problem behaviors. But when we look at the big picture, we see that although we scold or swat or shock, the learner stops for a moment but later repeats the same problem behavior, except now he only does the bad behavior when his owner isn't around. So we scold and swat, and they growl and lunge, and we scold and swat some more. A vicious cycle. Why do we keep on scolding and swatting? Because those actions usually interrupt the dog's problem behavior, and that interruption is valuable to us at that moment. However, by correcting the dog's behavior, we don't change how the dog will react to something aversive to him in the future. The dog will still growl, bark, lunge, and maybe bite.

But there is a more precise definition of punishment. When I use the word *punishment* from here on, it will be with this simple but scientific definition: punishment is a process through which a behavior is consistently followed by a consequence and, as a result, the behavior occurs less often in the future.

There's a behavior. There's a consequence, like a spanking. And the behavior happens less often after the behavior and consequence happen together.

That's punishment. It's the opposite of reinforcement. It destroys behavior rather than building it, and in the place of the destroyed behavior is an opening for something else. Anything else. Because punishment doesn't address the issue of what the dog should do instead. If the behavior continues to happen just as much in the future, it's not punishment. It's just a consequence that could be completely neutral and have absolutely no effect, or it could be something that makes the behavior stronger (reinforcement). Sometimes it could be a consequence that results in an increased rate of the behavior, and we're going to talk about that later. For now, if you don't see less of the behavior in the future, it's not punishment. And sometimes it can qualify as abuse.

Punishment can increase a dog's fear and make him more likely to behave aggressively.

Punishment happens naturally in the world all the time. Most of us only put a hand on a hot stove one time. *Boom.* Behavior punished. Sometimes we gradually stop hanging around with a grouchy person because the person keeps being grouchy to us. Behavior punished, just slower.

Most people are terrible at administering punishment to get the results they want. Although we often expect a dog's behavior to change because we punish him, the way we dole out punishment (or as traditional dog trainers say, *corrections*) isn't quite that reliable. Usually we do something harsh to our dog when he is behaving "badly," and this interrupts the behavior just long enough for us to get some relief. What happens in the future? Chances are, the problem behavior is going to happen again when the overall situation tells the dog that this behavior is going to get him the best results. The dog essentially risks a punishment from his momentarily insane owner to get a bigger reward: riddance of a terrifying stranger. Yes. Your dog may endure your corrections when he doesn't see any other option. He's not thinking very clearly at the moment. At the same time, he knows that sometimes his owner isn't insane. Sometimes his owner is great. But your dog doesn't have any reason to trust the stranger. You've got to convince him that trusting the person will be a safe thing to do.

To effectively eliminate problem behavior with punishment, you have to meet some specific criteria that are pretty hard to achieve.

1. You have to figure out what punishment method will work with your dog, and that presents a pile of problems right off the bat. You have to try out a bunch of different methods to see what will work on him. Do you hit him, shock him, put him in his crate for time out, or what? This is a big ethical challenge that could very easily turn into abuse, even though you truly love your dog. Next, you have to understand that what worked on your last dog may not work on this dog or may have a different effect on this dog. Your last dog may have just cut it out when you yelled at him once, and it was never an issue again. But the dog you have now may not be that easy. That doesn't make him a bad dog. That makes him a different dog.

2. You have to administer punishment immediately when the problem behavior happens. You can't wait until it's all over and you're walking back home to swat your dog for barking at a stranger and expect him to stop barking at strangers, right? All that will do is teach your dog that the walk home is going to be dangerous after he's been in a fight, which means that the walk home could become dangerous for you, too. You can't tell him, "Just you wait until your father gets home!" If you punish too late (or too soon), you're likely to punish the wrong behavior.

3. You have to punish if and only if the problem behavior happens, not when you make a mistake and shock at the wrong time, or when you think he was going to do something you want to punish but he was actually going to do something else. So, as you see, to use punishment effectively, you also have to be a doggy mind reader.

4. You have to punish as hard as necessary, but you have to do it while keeping those other criteria in place: use what works, do it right away, do it every time, only do it if he actually does the behavior (never if he doesn't), and do it hard enough to be effective. Ideally, you want the punishment to work so well that you only have to do it one time. Seriously. You have to punish the living daylights out of that aggressive lunge. Your heart will hurt 'til it bleeds, and it will definitely hurt your dog. Done precisely, the punishment can get rid of that problem behavior in that situation while opening a space for other problem behaviors to occur. But sufficient precision is incredibly difficult, success is not guaranteed, and it all comes with a lot of very big risks.

Many times, we start out with a light attempt at a correction: "Now, Buster, don't growl at Mr. Jones." Buster glances away, which makes us think it worked, but when he keeps growling at people on future walks, we move to threats

A large dog who tries to defend himself from punishment can cause a lot of damage.

(streams of intense words he doesn't understand), shouting, swatting, and worse. What does he do? He toughens up. He builds a tolerance to harsher and harsher punishments until they don't seem to faze him at all. That gradual escalation of intensity is how he learns to tolerate it; in this way, you are actually helping your dog build up a tolerance to aversive consequences. Try using physical punishment on a 150-pound Mastiff who has built up a tolerance to it—it's not going to be pretty. (Word to the wise: Start that Mastiff as a puppy with positive-reinforcement training and make cooperating with you fun so that you won't have to fight him when he's older and larger and in his prime.) It is far, far better to build desirable behavior with positive reinforcement than to think you can control your dog's behavior with force.

Effectiveness issues aside, using severe punishment on those who depend on you for everything is just not right. It's a big ethical and moral problem.

It's extraordinarily difficult to perform punishment correctly, and it's very easy to screw it up—not to mention that it's also a tragic breach of trust between you and your dog. A lot of times, a dog will respond to his punishing owner with submission by rolling onto his back, crouching, and crawling up to lick his owner under the chin, but this does not indicate that the dog thinks his owner is the best person ever. It means he knows he has to watch out for his owner. These behaviors mean that he's trying to convince his owner that while he might be a little like Cujo, he's basically a good dog and won't cause any trouble. He's saying, "Please don't hurt me." I'm sad to say that this happens with human children as well. I knew a foster mother who said that her foster children appreciated being spanked because they would approach her afterward, wanting to be held and saying, "I love you." It's the same thing. Those kids were trying to reinforce nonviolence in their caregiver because they were absolutely dependent on the safety that person represented.

You could argue that a hard, timely punishment that eliminates the problem behavior once and for all is, indeed, ethical, because it saves the dog from possible euthanasia, and it makes the family and community safer. There is logic to that. But there's one other ethical component to the decision to use punishment as a behavior-change tool. Dr. Richard Smith, associate professor and former department head of the Department of Behavior Analysis at the

University of North Texas taught that if you're going to resort to punishment, you must first (1) make sure you have tried all nonaversive techniques and (2) consult people who know behavior better than you do. And I assure you, there are people who know more than you do, no matter who you are. There's always someone.

Dr. Smith was talking about working with humans with severe behavior problems, but, from my point of view, the same criteria should apply to the aggressive dog. The dog can do a lot of harm, so people's lives and safety are at risk; typically, if he does attack, his life is then in danger, too. It's easy to go down to the pet-supply store and buy a shock collar and start shocking the dog for behaviors you don't like, but don't do it. It's not right

for stores to sell that stuff to begin with. If you find you are in a quandary about what to do instead, finish reading this book and work with a skilled trainer who knows how to work with aggressive dogs without the use of punishment. Punishment must be considered a last resort to be used only when all else has failed and only in partnership with a skilled trainer.

WHAT'S WRONG WITH SHOCK COLLARS

I've watched trainers use shock collars on their dogs. Of course, there are milder punishers than shock collars, and shock collars can be used at different intensities, but if we're going to talk about punishment, the shock collar is a clear example to use. You can watch this kind

In addition to being an aversive training method, using a shock collar does not teach the dog to associate the punishment with the bad behavior.

of training being performed—often quite poorly and for purposes that no shock should ever be needed for—on YouTube if you have the heart for it. If someone needs a shock collar to train a dog to heel, go into a crate, or sit, that person doesn't know what he or she is doing. If someone is repeatedly bitten by the dogs with whom he or she works, that person doesn't know what he or she is doing. Being bitten is a lot more common when you're in the practice of pushing your dog too hard.

When I was doing the CAT research with Dr. Rosales, a training colleague asked me to come with him to see some clients who had an aggressive German Shepherd Dog. This colleague told me in advance that the clients used shock collars on their dogs (they also had a Labrador Retriever) so that they could play in a field next to a busy highway. During the course of our afternoon together, the owners explained that the dogs didn't mind the shocks because whenever they brought the dogs'

collars out, the dogs knew it was playtime and would excitedly rush to the owners to have their collars put on.

To be honest, I doubted that the dogs liked their collars, but it turned out the owners were right. Their dogs did love their shock collars—a lot. I saw them get very excited and then very disappointed when the owners brought the collars out but then put them away.

"Do you shock the dogs as soon as you put their collars on them?"

"Of course not. They're only tapped if they get too close to the highway." *Tap* is a euphemism for shocking the dog. It came from the fact that pressing the button on the remote control for the collar is done with a tap of the thumb.

"Does it work?"

"Sure does! They avoid the edges of the field. They never go near the highway."

Do you see what I see? The dogs didn't learn to associate the sight of their shock collars with being shocked. They learned that they only get to go play in the big field full of sticks, lizards, smells, and lots of space to run when those collars are on, so, to the dogs, the collars are not shock collars, they're play-in-the-field collars. Again, the dogs did not associate their collars with shock; they associated them with the really fun field experience.

In those dogs' minds, the real risk occurred only at the edge of the field near the highway. They had learned that in order for things to stay fun, they should stay away from Shock Highway. They had learned to associate the highway with the shock. I must admit, that's the best use of a shock collar: setting up a bad association between the collar and something dangerous, such as rattlesnakes or busy highways or fun-to-chase calves that could die from being chased and overheated on a hot day. In Texas, that could easily cause the owner of said calves to shoot the dog. In these dogs' case, because the shock occurred when they got too close to the highway, they thought that the highway delivered the shock. Their collars are fun. The highway, not fun.

The owners had done a very good job making associations that helped them achieve the goal of being able to allow their dogs to play in a field that was really not a safe place to play. But, once in a while, something so enticing happens that a dog will endure a shock just to go get it. Sometimes the dog is so distracted that he forgets that the highway means shock. So he gets shocked and goes onto the highway anyway. Harsh punishment still isn't a sure thing.

My colleague and I didn't plan to use shock collars for training the aggressive dog (and, of course, we didn't), nor did we plan to work near the busy highway, so the German Shepherd was not wearing his shock collar when we arrived. The Labrador was completely friendly with

everyone, but the German Shepherd Dog hated dogs other than the Lab and was easily overwhelmed by people, so he was our client.

As we sat in the living room with the owners and discussed what previous work they had done on the dog's aggression, they admitted that, yes, they had used the German Shepherd Dog's shock collar to punish his aggression—but only after they had taken the dog to a football game, where a cheerleader had run up to him, squealed, and given him a big, sudden hug, and he had whipped around and bitten the girl right in the face. While the Labrador might have loved this attention, the German Shepherd did not. The girl required several stitches, and the dog was placed on home rabies quarantine for ten days. Texas laws allow some owners to quarantine their dogs at home, while other dogs must be turned over for quarantine in an animal control facility.

After the quarantine ended, the owners would strap on the German Shepherd's shock collar whenever they took him out in public—just in case. So, what do you think happened next? The owners zapped the dog for any perceived missteps, and his aggression got worse. They shocked him whenever they thought he acted as if he might behave aggressively toward a person or dog. His owners, who really loved their dog and had the best of intentions, wanted to interrupt the dog's behavior before it turned into a big, ugly, aggressive mess. So, if he looked at someone and stiffened, he got a shock. If he lowered his head slightly in the direction of another dog, he got a shock. In other words, when he saw a person or a dog, he got a shock.

The shock still wasn't associated with the collar in the dog's mind. Nor was it associated only with the highway anymore. Now, the dog began to associate the shock with other dogs and people. *Uh oh.* The very sight of people and dogs now set him off. He didn't just growl, he snarled, lunged, and tried to bite. He had gotten scary. His small female owner couldn't hold him back when he lunged, so she couldn't take him for walks by herself anymore, and she certainly couldn't walk the two dogs together. The muscular husband had enough trouble managing

the big guy himself. This was an adult male German Shepherd, in his prime, weighing more than 80 pounds and full of power.

Something you might have noticed here is that, earlier in the book, I said that you could start working on a dog's aggression by working with behaviors that occur earlier in the behavior chain. Interestingly, that doesn't seem to work with punishment. I don't know of any research to prove this, but it appears that when you punish a behavior, you might knock out just that one behavior, like growling. But if you use reinforcement, you can eliminate the whole chain. Why? Because with the kind of reinforcement I'm going to teach you, which involves reinforcing behavior you like and not reinforcing behavior you don't like, a dog learns what to do instead, and he doesn't have to go through his whole bag of tricks, up to and including the bite. He just

This dog's expression demonstrates the anxiety of always being at risk of being shocked.

turns his head. He just sits. He just does something else.

I asked if I could see the German Shepherd Dog's shock collar. The wife handed it to me. As I mentioned, the dogs got very excited and were then sorely disappointed when we did not end up going for a walk. I asked if it was on the setting they used for the German Shepherd. Yes, it was, although they had started out using it at a lower setting and then increased the intensity over time as it grew less effective. Remember what I wrote earlier about building up a tolerance? Settings vary on different models of shock collars, but this one was set at 6 on a dial that went up to 10.

I asked if they would mind if I discharged the collar on myself. Everyone got very quiet, including my colleague.

"I just want to see what he experiences," I said.

The female owner said, "Are you sure?" Yikes. They were concerned for my well-being when this was something they did to their dogs all the time. But, granted, I was a fluffy middle-aged mom, not an athlete or a German Shepherd Dog in his prime. I left some quiet space in the room for a moment to see if they wanted to offer any more information. I also kind of wished they'd give me a compelling reason or two not to do it.

I asked, "Have you ever been shocked by this collar?"

"No."

I repeated, "Is this the setting it's on when your dog wears it?"

"Yes," they replied quietly.

"Are you OK with me doing it?"

Deep breaths from the owners. I think my colleague held his breath, too.

"OK," they said. The wife took a couple of steps backward. My colleague's eyes were as big as saucers. The husband crossed his arms. I think he wanted to think it was funny.

I placed the collar's two electrified probes against the inside of my left forearm. The two probes touch the skin, and the electricity travels through the probes and then passes through the body. I took a deep breath and pressed the button on the remote control. A shock went through my entire body—not just my forearm, but my entire body. I had an immediate urge to vomit. My consciousness "left the room" for a couple of seconds. I don't know how to explain it other than to say that because of the pain I had just experienced, I wasn't really "there" momentarily.

For the rest of that day and into the next, I was nauseated and unable to eat. This was from one shock at a setting slightly above the halfway mark on the dial. I wonder how many dogs experience the full power of these devices over and over again. If the Internet is any indicator, it's a lot.

After we left the training session, my colleague told me a story about a dog trainer friend of his. He was a former Marine who was experienced with dogs and was not naïve. He once did something quite similar to what I had just done and shocked himself with a dog's shock collar in front of other people. He wet his pants.

"I thought you were going to soak their couch!"

"That was a very real possibility," I said.

What was happening here was that this dog got a sharp shock every time something worrisome crossed his line of sight. The instant he saw a teenage girl who bore some vague resemblance to the hugging cheerleader, he would tense up. Maybe he thought she was getting ready to come and hug him. He knew he'd better keep an eye on her. If she did happen to walk in his direction, his behavior would intensify, and zap! What did we expect the dog to learn? He learned that electronic zaps to the neck are more likely in the presence of teenage girls. The dog made the same association in the presence of anything he got shocked for looking at.

So, if this zap is truly punishment in the scientific sense—if it really reduces the behavior—why is it a problem? If it actually works and makes him stop aggressing, why not shock him? That seems to be a common philosophical question in the training world, and it's a good one. Countercontrol is one reason. *Countercontrol* means that the dog who keeps getting punished will eventually fight back. When I was a young adult in New Orleans, I volunteered at the SPCA of Greater New Orleans. The bad guy's dog of choice back then was the Doberman. People would say that you couldn't trust Dobermans because they would turn on their owners. Well, guess what? That wasn't about the breed. That was about countercontrol. The dogs were punished again and again until they fought back. They did turn on their owners, but not because of their breed. They turned on their owners because they were taught that it was their only option.

What about the risk of building associations between the shock and more and more things that the dog really needs to live in peace with? Yeah, that's a problem, too. What about the fact that the dog may shut down when he knows that his variety of warning behaviors are going to result in a shock but that, if he gets close enough, he still might bite? If the teenager comes close enough, the German Shepherd might decide it's worth the risk of a shock to deal with this very real and present danger. This happens more often than you might think.

Shouting, yanking on the dog's leash, pulling the dog forcibly away by the collar, and other seemingly lesser punitive techniques, or corrections, work the same way. Shocking is just one example. If bad things happen to a dog in the presence of—anything—it's possible that thing is going to become a sign to the dog that trouble is a-brewin'. It doesn't matter whether it's a teenage girl or a kid on a skateboard or a man with a knife poised in *Psycho* position above his head. A dog's gotta do what a dog's gotta do, even if he doesn't understand the big picture. It doesn't matter that the hugging cheerleader didn't mean any harm, or that the man who freaked him out on his morning walks was merely chronically late for work, resulting in his daily sudden bursts out his front door, and that both are harmless to dogs. It just matters that these dogs developed bad associations with these people/events, and aggression became the best weapon in their arsenals.

4
BE PRESENT: HOW TO OBSERVE ACCURATELY

> **I just sit back and observe. You learn more that way.**
>
> **~ Sonya Teclai**

This chapter is a workshop. To prepare for the work you will do, I recommend that you go ahead and read the rest of the book and then return to this chapter. It is essential for you to learn how to understand what you are seeing when you watch your dog. As we've already discussed, your dog will behave in some ways just like other dogs, and he will do other things in his own unique way. Instead of giving you a cookie-cutter list of safe versus aggressive behaviors, I'm going to help you make your own list specifically for your dog.

You'll need a notebook, smart phone, or computer so you can record your responses to the questions and exercises throughout the chapter. If you want to read through the entire chapter before starting to take notes, that is fine. Make your notes as soon after you observe your dog's behavior as possible. It's very easy to forget and then inadvertently mentally edit what we thought we saw. If you can record your dog's behavior, you're ahead of the game because you can watch the video as many times as needed. It's important to note that you should not try to get your dog to act in any certain way for these observations, and you should not put him in situations he will find difficult.

What does your dog do when he's aggressive? What does your dog do when he's friendly?

Instead of thinking of biting as aggressive behavior, just think of biting as biting, and do the same for all other behaviors. Did he bite or not? Did he growl or not? Did he lunge or not? Did he lower his ears? Pull back his lips? Drool? Scratch his neck?

What specific behavior does your dog do that is causing problems?

Don't worry about whether he is scared or mad. Just watch him in his everyday life and note what you see him actually doing. He barks. He lunges. He tries to hide, and if your nephew corners him, he lunges. He pushes your neighbor hard with his paws and barks in his face.

You might notice some more subtle behaviors. He holds his breath. (This is harder to see in fluffy dogs, but there's often a place in the body where you can see it, such the neck, the nostrils, or the mouth.) You can break that down a bit more, and instead of saying that he's holding his breath, you could note that his belly tightened or his nostrils stopped moving. Maybe you see his tongue go inside his mouth and his mouth close. He might lick his lips. He might shake off as if he were wet, but he's completely dry. He might yawn even though he's not tired. Does he stare? Does he do something that seems completely benign but is always or often followed by something worrisome, like a growl, lunge, or attempted bite? Does he lower his head or back up? The first part of your task at this phase is to learn to simply see what your dog does.

You may have ideas about why your dog behaves aggressively. Maybe it seems like he wants to protect you, and maybe that's true. You may have been told that he is dominant or he is territorial. Maybe he was bred to be aggressive, or maybe he is stubborn and uncooperative. Maybe you believe he was abused. Maybe he wasn't well socialized as a pup, meaning that his owners didn't introduce him to a variety of safe, fun experiences, so everything new seems scary to him. Sometimes we know a dog's history, and sometimes we don't, but, either way, we can still work with him. Knowing these reasons behind your dog's behavior might be helpful, but focusing too much on the reasons, especially when you are only speculating, can make your work with your dog less effective. What matters is that your dog is doing something that isn't safe for others or for himself.

As you prepare yourself to work with your dog, you must practice observing. There are some techniques that are critical for performing CAT well and safely. The observation techniques I will teach you are very important. They will help you better understand your dog and make the very best decisions for him.

You've been watching your dog for as long as you've had him. You may have tons of pictures of him on your phone. You may have logged a lot of miles walking together or hours on the couch, watching movies together. My goal is to teach you how to really and truly observe your dog wherever he is and whatever he is doing so that you can understand what you're seeing without either reading too much into it or excusing it. Reading too much into it might be, "Oh no! He growled! He's not safe, and I can't keep him." Excusing it might be, "Oh, he's just playing."

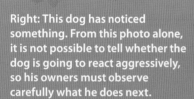

Right: This dog has noticed something. From this photo alone, it is not possible to tell whether the dog is going to react aggressively, so his owners must observe carefully what he does next.

Below: As a dog gets closer to aggressive behavior, it's common for him to pull the corners of his mouth closer to the front to form a C shape and keep his tongue inside his mouth, as shown. The aggression at this point is mild; there is no visible tightness in his facial muscles.

We had some friends years ago whose Weimaraner roared loudly into my husband's face every time my husband sneezed. The dog would run to my husband, and there was so much energy behind his roars that his front feet left the ground. Sometimes he even threw in a shove with his front paws. One of his owners would drag him away by the collar each time this happened. The family thought it was just "Harley being Harley." Yeah, I guess it was, but Harley was a pretty scary dog. You've got to learn to see what your dog does and take it at face value. Had these owners been clients, I might have asked, "Did he bark into Richard's face? Is that something you want to continue? Was it a safe, friendly behavior?"

Many books on dog aggression will tell you about canine communication signals and how to read canine body language. You need to know this information, and it is very valuable as far as learning about the canine species. Your very important job right now,

This dog is demonstrating calm, attentive behavior. What he does before and after this behavior will tell his owner more about whether he will behave aggressively. Remember, chains of behaviors give valuable information about how your dog is most likely to behave next.

though, is to learn about your individual dog. He is part of a species and a breed (or more than one breed); as such, he will have many behaviors in common with other dogs. Your dog also is an individual with his own collection of experiences from which he has learned. You can't assume that your dog is going to do exactly what dogs are supposed to do. There are some diagrams used by dog trainers that list the behaviors dogs exhibit as their stress levels escalate from relaxation to aggression. I wanted to get a better handle on how I could use these charts, so in preparing to write this book, I made ten chronological ethograms based on videos of dogs, including a few dogs with whom I'd worked. A chronological ethogram is a chart of behaviors, listed in the order they occur. Because I have personally worked with many aggressive dogs over the past decade, I had created my own imaginary ethogram in my head. I was pretty sure that dogs performed aggressive behaviors in roughly this order:

1. Sense presence of thing he's concerned about (person, other dog, etc.) in some way (sight, sound, etc.)
2. Notice or look at it
3. Freeze (hold very still)
4. Close mouth
5. Pull tongue inside mouth
6. Lower head
7. Put ears back
8. Push corners of lips forward, closer to nose
9. Back up or bend back legs
10. Move forward quickly
11. Launch toward person or dog
12. Bite

This, or something similar, is what I believed I saw nearly every time a dog behaved aggressively.

What do you think I found with my small study of ten dogs? In my small, casual study, no dog performed all of those behaviors. Most threw in extra behaviors; for example, one dog always turned in a complete circle before lunging. And they never did the behaviors in precisely this order. Dogs mix it all up. In the ten dogs I watched, their behaviors were similar, but not identical. You can't even guarantee that the same dog will perform exactly the same behaviors every time.

Your dog probably hasn't studied the diagrams that trainers use. He does what he has learned to do based on what is worthwhile to him at a moment in time in a given situation. And while he doesn't intend it, he will likely do the textbook things from time to time, even if he doesn't do them exactly the way they're laid out in diagrams. So I discarded the idea of either borrowing an established diagram or creating my own generalized diagram. There needs to be one diagram per dog per experience. You've got to watch your own dog and get to know what

he does in situations where his aggressive behaviors occur.

EXERCISE 1

Practice this exercise for short periods of time (two to ten minutes) as often as you can every day. It's better to do a short session every day than to do a longer session once or twice a week. Get into the habit of doing this regularly—you can do anything for two minutes!

This is an observation practice for you, with your dog as the focus. One of the most common things trainers and behaviorists hear about dog bites is that they came out of the blue with no warning. That often seems true, but it never is. There was a warning, but it's very common for people to miss the warnings either because they're not in the habit of

This dog's teeth and puckered upper lip suggest that he is behaving aggressively, but how can you tell for sure? Observe what happens before and after this behavior.

Yawns are not just for tired dogs. They often occur when a dog is learning and are appropriate behaviors to reinforce instead of aggression.

watching their dogs' behavior or because they don't understand what they're seeing.

I once observed a couple of rescue puppies from Korea who had been transported to the United States for adoption. These two young Jindo puppies were surprisingly well adjusted, and they are both now enjoying good lives with adoptive families. But when they first arrived at the shelter, someone approached with a camera with a large flash attachment on it and began to snap photos of them. The puppies backed up, lowered their heads, and barked. The photographer said, "Well, at least they're being playful." I explained that the pups were expressing fear. They had never seen a camera before, much less one with such a large light attachment (I don't think I'd ever seen one of those before, either).

To me, it was obvious that the puppies were reacting to try to escape this huge thing they'd never seen before. This was true reactivity—they were alarmed by

this massive space-age device that was flashing bright light at them. Had it continued, they certainly would have kept barking, and they were already retreating to try and hide. Fortunately, the photographer was a kind, animal-loving person who quickly changed her tactic upon hearing what the pups were experiencing, and the puppies quickly recovered their normal friendly behavior. But the fact is, despite being an animal lover, this photographer didn't understand what the puppies were saying with their body language.

Most people don't understand what their dogs are telling them with their responses to their environments, and that's understandable. No one teaches us; it's something we have to make an effort to learn, which we only do if it somehow becomes clear that we need to take action. Fortunately for most of us, most dogs don't require a lot of fancy knowledge. They fit in with their families pretty well. But it's not uncommon for dogs to do things that are problematic. That's when we have to take a step back and study up before taking the next step.

In this exercise, don't expect anything in particular to happen; you're just seeing what your individual dog does in the situations he finds himself in. You're just being aware of your dog living his life. Because aggression is such a big deal, it is very important for you to learn how to observe carefully and to really notice what is happening. It's hard to do that in the middle of your dog's aggressive flare-up, so we're going to start practicing when he's feeling at ease and both of you are in a comfortable situation.

Grab your computer or your notebook and pen and have it beside you; you will need it for subsequent exercises. Turn off the sound on your phone, turn it over so that you can't see notifications, and put it down. If you will be taking notes on your phone, turn off the notifications and silence ringtones so that you can focus on this observation. If you normally have the TV or computer on, turn the volume down but leave it on so that it won't seem strange to the dog. Turn away from the TV or computer so that you aren't distracted.

Sit in a chair with your back straight and your feet on the floor. This position will help you tune in completely. You need to be in an alert position, not a position that will make it hard for you to pay attention.

First, just sit in this position. Don't pay particular attention to your dog right now. Just be aware of this place and time. Does your back hurt? (Move around a little to get comfortable.) Are your feet cold? Do

Averting the eyes and turning the head are among common behaviors to reinforce in place of aggression.

you feel a pleasant breeze from a window? What sounds do you hear? What do you see right in front of you? Just notice these things. Your dog can be in the room, but do not give him any commands or gestures. Just let him do what he chooses to do; if he is crated, just leave him as he is.

Even though this part sounds pretty simple, it will probably take some practice. You're going to get distracted at first, and that's OK. You're just practicing. Just notice the distraction and go back to being aware and present in your space.

Take a deep breath and exhale in a normal, natural way. There's no need to do fancy yoga breathing. You're just firing up your brain to do its best work. As you get comfortable and start to relax, your breathing may slow. Let it. Let your body manage the right amount of oxygen so that your brain can pay attention to your dog.

Do this every day for a couple of minutes. You can move right into Exercise 2 from this exercise, or you can do them separately.

EXERCISE 2

Be sure that you can see your dog from where you are sitting. If you can't, move to a place in the room where you can see him, sit down again as previously described, and have your notebook near you. Take a gentle look at your dog. Don't stare at him, and avoid keeping your eyes glued to his face. If his body tenses or he stares back, move your eyes away from his face, look at the floor, and turn your head slightly to either side. Relax your face and

eyes and watch him gently. For some dogs, it may be helpful to look at his paw or shoulder or rump rather than straight at his face, or to move your eyes from place to place on his body.

Watch what your dog is doing. Did his behavior change when you started watching him? What did he do? In your notebook, write the following and jot down a couple of notes about what he did: When I started watching him, he (e.g., stood up and stretched, came to me, wagged his tail, continued sleeping, etc.).

For each of the following components of Exercise 2, jot down quick notes:

- Pick up your phone and observe what he does for one minute.
- Turn to face your computer or TV while watching him from the corner of your eye. What does he do when you change your activity?
- Walk to the kitchen. What does he do?
- Experiment with a few common tasks around the house, such as sweeping the floor, wiping down the counters, and stretching out on the couch. What does he do as you do each of these things?

If you're like most modern humans, you are focused on technology until something in the environment changes. You want a glass of water, so you get up, and your dog follows you. You pet him on the head. He either nudges you to do it some more, jumps on you, turns his head away, or does something completely different. Or maybe you just sit down in your chair, and he comes out of a slumber and thumps his tail, so you stroke his ears or scratch his neck.

Ready to pounce or ready to play? Again, observation is the key.

Did you know that we cannot pay attention to two things at once? When we are messing with our phones and watching our dogs at the same time, we are actually switching back and forth between the two things, so we really aren't getting a clear picture of either one. I am notorious for watching TV while checking Facebook or reading an article on my phone. I often miss a pertinent part of the show or skim through an article without really absorbing it. But when you have an aggressive dog, you can't afford to divide your attention in many situations. You have to be on your game.

As you record your observations, realize that there are no correct answers; there are only observations. Take note of what he actually did. These notes will be useful and interesting to refer to as you go through the work we're going to talk about.

EXERCISE 3

For the purposes of learning your dog's behavior, I encourage you to think about it in terms that other people are most likely to agree with if they see your dog in action. If you say to Joe, your neighbor, "Don't worry; my dog is friendly," Joe may think you're nuts because his experience may be different. Maybe Joe is one of the people your dog barks at every day. Joe may be suspicious of every move your Fido makes. If you're on a walk and your dog pounces when he sees Joe, you may think, "Oh, he's feeling playful," but Joe may think, "That darn dog lunged at me again!" You're both describing the same behavior, but both you and Joe have edited your memories and interpretations of what Fido did, and you have each labeled his actions in a way that fits with your experience. That's not fair to Fido, even if you're the one saying he's friendly. If you think your dog is friendly, yet he lunges at people, you are missing the cues your dog has been giving you that he is uncomfortable and is moving closer to behaving in a way that may be risky and dangerous. Remember, if there's risk to a human or another dog, there's risk to your dog, too. Humans don't tolerate aggression from dogs very well, and someone could report your dog to authorities[1].

EXERCISE 4

Here's a way to get your brain around describing your dog's behavior. Think about a hat and describe it to yourself. Don't read any further until you have that hat in mind and write down some notes or draw it in your notebook.

Me? I instantly thought of a tweed flat cap my Dad used to wear. It was a brown

---

1   Don't blame the authorities, though. Their job is to uphold the law and keep the community safe.

and rust-colored houndstooth pattern on an off-white background. The back was a bit taller than the front. It had a narrow brim in the front. How about your hat? Ask your family or a few people on social media to describe or post a picture of the first hat they think of.

How similar are the hats you, your friends, and I described? The first response I got when I posted this on Facebook was "Made of twigs, adorning a beautiful woman of a certain age." It was accompanied by a photographic art piece of an elderly woman wearing a huge headdress made of twigs. Some other people posted knit caps in a variety of colors and there were a couple of fedoras and some baseball caps with different logos on them. There was a hat shaped like a Christmas tree, another was a Cat in the Hat-style hat, and another was a 1950s pillbox hat with a small mesh veil like Jackie O used to wear. Big hats, little hats,

red hats, and blue hats, most everyone thought of a different type of hat.

The hat we think of first may change from day to day. If you asked me on a different day to describe a hat, I would think of a straw cowboy hat I found in my son's room as we moved things out to prepare for installing new flooring.

All of these different descriptions means that *hat* isn't descriptive enough. It's too general. If I tell you I want a hat, but you don't know it's because I'm cold so you buy me a Jackie O pillbox hat, I'm still going to have cold ears. The context is important. So, I would probably get a more appropriate hat if I said, "I'm cold. Do you have a knit cap I could borrow?" It's important to work on our clarity and create some clear definitions.

So, let's say Fido pounces at Joe, and Joe freaks out. You think Fido is friendly and cute, and you can't figure out why Joe is acting this way. Joe thinks your dang dog is terrifying. How do we clarify what your dog actually did? To clarify, we think about behavior instead of labels, and we think of behaviors in context. Behaviors are things you can observe happening in a certain situation, and the practice in this exercise will help you get better at reading them.

This may sound kind of simplistic, but your dog's behavior is anything your dog can do, and, for the purposes of our observations, anything you can see him doing. Examples include walk, sit, lift a paw, hold tail stiffly above his spine level, wag tail slowly and loosely below his spine, make a panting noise, extend tongue from his mouth, dig a hole in the garden, grab the pot roast off the kitchen counter.

Friendly is a very general label that isn't too helpful and is not a specific behavior at all. It's a general way to describe a group of behaviors. I think my dog is friendly, but is that a universal view? My dog, Aero, wags his tail in a helicopter circle and puts his head on a lot of people's chests. He did that with my sister, and he did that with a former boss the very first time he met her. But several years ago, a man approached my office door with a former boss. When Aero saw the man, he froze, growled, and barked loudly. I was shocked. I had never seen this behavior from him before. But now I know that my dog may put his head on some people's chests in some situations, but he may also growl and bark at some other people in some other situations. Is my dog friendly? Yes, sometimes. And no, sometimes. Context is key.

Going forward, in your observation notebook, jot down not only what your dog does but also the context in which he does it. In my book, I might have two notes.

In my living room, my dog placed his head on my sister's chest and wagged his tail in a circle.

In my office, my dog growled and lunged at an animal cruelty investigator.

It's perfectly fine to use expressions like *friendly* and *aggressive* in general conversation. If we didn't use words like those, it would take forever to tell a story. But for observation purposes, if the expression doesn't describe the behavior and situation in a way that allows everyone to understand what happened, don't use it. We need to know whether we're talking Stetsons or swim caps.

EXERCISE 5

Create a log in your notebook with the following headings:

Number
Date and Time
Dog's Activity before Behavior
Situation
Who Was There?
Dog's Activity after Behavior

Under *Number*, number the incidents as they occur during the day. Under *Date and Time,* include the time of day or night when you made the observation. Under *Dog's Activity before/after Activity*, record simply and clearly what the dog did as you learned to do in the earlier observation exercises. Under *Situation*, indicate where and when the behavior happened and what circumstances might have been related to the behavior's happening. In the *Who Was There?* column, indicate who else (people and animals) was there when the behavior happened. Log information daily, and don't limit your observations to aggressive behavior only.

Dogs who want to keep the peace will often avert their eyes. If an aggressive dog chooses this, we should reward it.

OBSERVING WITHOUT LABELING

Let's do another short observation of your dog and describe what he is actually doing, without labels. You're going to start the same way as in previous exercises. Get in your upright position with your feet on the floor, and take some deep breaths until you feel comfortable. Take a few more breaths. Look at your dog in the way I instructed you earlier. What did he do this time?

I did this exercise with Aero, and here's my observation:

When I turned to look at him, Aero was lying on the floor. His back legs were extended to his left side with his weight on his right hip. His front legs were extended in front of him and his upper body was upright and sternal (on the keel of his chest) with his weight balanced on his elbows. His head was resting on his left front leg. His eyes were already aimed at me when I looked at him. He lifted his head and began to lick his left front leg, making an audible slurping noise. As I continued to look at him, he lifted his head and chewed at a spot behind his shoulder blade for a second before lifting his left back leg to scratch his neck. He looked at me, the whites of his eyes showing, and scratched some more. He turned his head away from me, yawned with a wide-open mouth, and closed his mouth quickly, resulting in his teeth making a clacking sound. He rested his head on his leg and smacked his lips twice. As I turned back to my computer, I heard a fairly loud exhale through his nose.

What's the first thing you thought as you read that? If you read my description and

Is the dog feeling uncomfortable or simply scratching an itch?

thought that Aero sounded uncomfortable, I would have to agree. It wasn't what I expected him to do; I thought he would get up and come over to me. I was wrong. My observation was right. Later, as you perform these exercises over and over, you will become more accurate in your predictions, but you'll still miss sometimes. Why is that? It's often because something in the environment that you're not tuned into has changed. Some changes in the environment are very subtle, so they can be hard to catch. In the case of my observation of Aero, I think he wasn't used to me turning around from my computer and just looking at him—so I was the part of the environment that had changed. He wasn't uncomfortable enough to bark or run away, and because he has a good, long history with me, he probably wasn't worried that I'd suddenly attack him.

Think about how it feels to have someone start staring at you. It can be uncomfortable. Aero's licking his leg audibly, chewing a spot behind his shoulder blade, scratching his neck, showing the whites of his eyes, and yawning are all behaviors that sometimes indicate stress in dogs. But he might do the same things if he were covered in fleas, right? So we have to cover all our bases.

In my notebook, I could write that my observation made Aero a little nervous (a general label) or, to use an expression common in dog training, that he was displaying a lot of *calming signals*, (another label)[2]. Or I could simply refer to what I wrote in the paragraph describing his behavior. Which description of his behavior is clearer? *Nervous* is a label that can describe a lot of different behaviors and could mean a lot of different things to different people. Scratching himself could suggest stress or it could indicate fleas. Aero did what he did, so that is what I described. If I said he was nervous because I was looking at him, you would have to figure out your own explanations for what I meant. But when you read the paragraph in which I described what Aero did, how much did you have to figure out about his behavior? Nothing, I hope.

You must learn to see the behaviors that are part of *your* dog's behavior chain when he's heading toward dangerous behavior, and this exercise teaches you how to observe behavior. Do Exercise 5 often. Don't do it only when you think your dog is going to behave aggressively or just after he behaved aggressively. Start with just doing it whenever, wherever. Do it for varying lengths of time, in different locations, with different things going on, and at different times of day. You can do it anytime you're with your dog.

Remember to look for the specific behaviors you see, not the labels. Then look for chains of behavior that seem to be hooked together in a particular order.

Do you see your dog performing the same behaviors in a similar consecutive series in similar situations? For example, when you turn to look at him, does he lift his lead, lick his leg, scratch his neck, and yawn? Does he keep it mixed up? What does he do? Practice watching a lot.

Eventually, you're going to need to find what your dog does as he gears up to behave aggressively. Doing Exercise 5 frequently during neutral times is going to help you learn to see his behavior in context. When behavior scientists study behavior, one of the key things they are working toward is to be able to predict when a behavior is likely to happen. You are a researcher in this process. Instead of me telling you what your dog is going to do next, it's essential for you to learn how to predict it yourself. Learn how to describe your dog's particular behavior chains clearly. To predict aggressive behaviors with the most accuracy possible, you have to know what your dog will do, not what the textbook dog will do. Your dog is a unique, individual canine.

2   *On Talking Terms with Dogs: Calming Signals* is a book by Norwegian dog expert Turid Rugaas in which she describes some common behaviors related to dogs interacting with others. Her book can help you identify behaviors of significance.

5

UNDERSTAND YOUR DOG'S AGGRESSIVE OR REACTIVE BEHAVIOR

> **The dog has seldom been successful in pulling man up to its level of sagacity, but man has frequently dragged the dog down to his.**
>
> **~ James Thurber**

There is so much folklore about dogs, and we are so fully steeped in it from the time we first utter the syllable "dog" as young children, that it can be very difficult to tease apart what is fact and what is fairy tale. Whether this is your first dog or your fifty-seventh, you have heard that you have to be your dog's leader, that dogs smell fear, that dogs are pack animals, that dogs are descended from wolves. Am I right? There are elements of truth to all of these views of the nature of a dog, but the extent to which these truisms aren't the whole story can cause us problems when we need to change our dog's behavior. This is especially true when our dog is performing risky, aggressive behaviors. They also don't take into account what a dog learns in his lifetime. *Nature* and *nurture* are part of the same whole.

There are some kinds of behavior you don't have to learn. Let's say a piece of dust blows into your eye, and you blink. No one had to give you lessons on blinking in that situation; you just did it because that's how your body is made. This is how many people look at aggression. A person walks in front of a dog, and the dog lunges and bites. The person thinks the dog is hardwired to behave aggressively just as we are hardwired to blink. This is an incomplete view of the behavior.

The very respected animal trainer Bob Bailey likes to say that Pavlov is always sitting on your shoulder. You've likely heard of Pavlov, the twentieth-century biologist who started out performing studies on the digestive systems of dogs. In the process, he observed that once the dogs received food from a researcher in a white lab coat several times, the dogs would begin to salivate when they saw the lab coat, even if they didn't get any food. Pavlov figured out that this pairing of items that were once neutral objects (a lab coat or a bell) with something that was essential for survival (food) resulted in the dogs' displaying biological responses to food when they saw the guy in the white lab coat or heard that bell.

Animal trainers grabbed on to this principle and started using it to change dogs' emotional states. For example, if a dog was aggressive toward men, the dog would be given a piece of food every time he sees a man, with the goal of conditioning him to associate the man with the yummy treat. This process is called *classical conditioning* (or, in modern jargon, *respondent conditioning*). Procedures using this knowledge are practiced extensively in the rehabilitation of dogs with reactivity and aggression as well as with other species and humans. "Pavlov is on your shoulder" means that, when training animals, we have to remember that classical conditioning is taking place all the time. When the dogs saw the guy with the white lab coat, they naturally salivated because of their past association with the guy in the lab coat and food. A modern trainer offers small treats when a reactive or aggressive dog sees another dog or a person, with the goal of conditioning the dog to feel good when he sees the dog or person instead of feeling aggressive or afraid.

Dr. Rosales used to say, "Yes, Pavlov is sitting on one shoulder, and Skinner is sitting on the other." B. F. Skinner is the psychologist who founded the field of behavior analysis. Dr. Skinner (who reportedly preferred for his students to call him Fred) identified operant conditioning as a process that takes place naturally in the world, just like classical conditioning. Operant conditioning was the name he gave to learning based on the consequences for the behavior in a certain situation. The outcome may be reinforcing, meaning that it makes the behavior

stronger (e.g., the dog sits, you give him a treat, and he is more likely to sit in your presence in the future), or it can be punishing (e.g., the dog sits, a loud siren goes off outside, and the dog is less likely to sit in your presence again). *Operant*

BOB BAILEY

Bob Bailey (1936–) completed his bachelor's degree in zoology in 1959 and later studied computer programming. He holds four patents for electromechanical devices for animal training and for use in educational and amusement displays, and he has trained at least 120 species. In 1962, he became the director of animal training for the U.S. Navy. In 1965, Bailey became the assistant technical director, and later the vice president and general manager, of Animal Behavior Enterprises (ABE), working with Keller and Marian Breland, where he headed programs for the Department of Defense and all of the marine mammal programs. During his time with the Navy and ABE, much of his work was classified. Bob married Marian Breland in 1976 (Keller Breland had died years earlier), and they continued traveling and teaching about behavior and technology. In 1990, he became CEO of Eclectic Science Productions, a position he still held at the time of this writing.

behavior is behavior that happens because it is followed by a desirable consequence (a reinforcer), resulting in the animal doing that behavior more often in the future.

Many people believe that aggression is primarily about inherited traits, but according to the research I conducted under Dr. Rosales's direction, aggression is operant behavior. When the aggressive behavior happened, it produced a consequence that the dog wanted. Before we started CAT with the dog, the dog's aggression made something he didn't like go away or stop happening. That consequence made the dog willing to be aggressive again. During the process of CAT, the dog learned that if he did nicer things, the thing he didn't like would still go away or stop, so there

was no point in getting all worked up about it. And when we completed CAT training from beginning to end, the dog completely changed his mind about the thing he didn't like, and now he acted friendly toward it. So we're back to the beginning, where an association changed the emotional response of the dog. He didn't have to get mad or scared anymore because he knew he could control his world with friendly behavior.

Many trainers believe that they can manage but not change aggression because it is something inherent in the dog (a blink when there's dust in your eye) instead of something the dog learned (you are more likely to get a treat if you sit for your owner). However, while it's true that a dog may have been startled the first time he saw a stranger on the sidewalk, if he reflexively growled and that stranger went away—*aha!*—the dog got a desirable outcome. He got something good out of it.

Our research showed that we could use the same outcome that taught the dog to exhibit aggressive behavior in the first place to reinforce safer and friendlier behaviors—different behaviors than those the dog had chosen. What we discovered was that *increasing distance* from the scary or otherwise aversive thing made the dog do certain behaviors over and over. *If I see a scary guy and I growl, he runs away. Check. I'm going to try that again next time.* We know these dogs' behaviors are susceptible to distance as a reward because we tried it many times with different dogs as well as many times with the same dog. The dogs learned to behave in ways people define as aggressive because their behavior chased the scary or bothersome things away. But guess what? If the scary or bothersome thing went away when they did nice things, they did more nice things. What we had to do was figure out a training situation where we could show them that choosing different behaviors would work for them, and that they would achieve the desired outcome when they behaved nicely, not when they behave aggressively.

Dr. Rosales had already been working with students on similar projects for several years before I came along. The first project I participated in involved some fearful but nonaggressive llamas. We waited for a llama to do something we wanted him to do, like take a step toward us, then we dropped a treat and walked away. It was quite effective, although the animals didn't always eat the treats. Stressed-out animals often can't eat. In the CAT research, we didn't bother with treats because we learned that we can purposefully use distance to reinforce nicer behaviors over aggressive ones without food. Food is not useful if the dog is too upset to eat it.

You are going to identify the good behaviors you want to see instead of the undesirable behaviors by doing the observations in Chapter 4. You will create clear descriptions of your dog's behavior like those that you practiced in

A treat when the dog sits reinforces, or strengthens, the desired behavior of sitting.

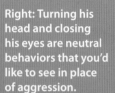

your observation exercises. The dog was not doing "nothing" during that break between aggressive actions. He was doing something else. What was it? Sniffing the ground? Turning his head? Looking at his owner? Lying down? Walking away? Stretching? The dog's interim behaviors are what we are going to reinforce and what we want to see more of. We are going to create a training situation in which the aversive person or dog moves away while the dog is exhibiting benign behaviors instead of while the dog is behaving aggressively (don't worry; we will take appropriate safety precautions). We will teach the dog that behaving aggressively will no longer work to get the scary guy to go away, but doing other, safer things will.

Many positive trainers are concerned about the stress this causes a dog. This is a valid and very important point.

All of the training methods that work to reduce or eliminate aggression are stressful on dogs because dogs have to be exposed to things that make them uncomfortable to learn how to be comfortable around them. With humans, a therapist might ask a person to imagine something he or she is scared of at first instead of immediately exposing the person to the real thing, but we don't know how to do this with dogs. Many modern trainers don't want their dogs to experience stress, but my view is that we want to introduce minimal stress and show the dog that he can easily change the unpleasant situation. You, as the owner and trainer, will be responsible for setting the situation up in such a way that he can do this. Learning algebra in school is stressful. Learning to swim is stressful. Learning to trust behaviors other than aggression when aggression has worked well for you is stressful. But, rest assured, this procedure will not put any more pressure on the dog than necessary and, in fact, is designed to minimize stress while the dog is learning to trust the effectiveness of his new behavior.

When we were doing the original CAT research, I made some videos that showed dogs going "over threshold," meaning that the dog became stressed to the point that he behaved aggressively. Alas, there are four points I want to make about this.

First, for the purposes of demonstrating our work, we often selected videos of aggression incidents to show what we did when aggressive behavior inadvertently happened. It looked like there were many trials in which the dog was pushed too hard. That was misleading. There were many, many more trials in which the dogs did not respond aggressively.

Second, desensitization and counterconditioning, the procedures used by excellent modern trainers, also sometimes result in aggressive responses, so assuming that CAT is unique in that respect is untrue. It goes back to the point I made a moment ago that these dogs are learning something new, and learning is stressful. Sometimes you accidentally get your dog too close to something that worries him. Sometimes something you haven't identified or controlled changes in the environment. Or sometimes your dog decides to try barking louder and harder because he wants to see if it will work if he is more enthusiastic. There's stress involved in learning. There just is.

Third, I humbly admit I was pretty new to training dogs at that point. I started training with an aggressive Moluccan cockatoo in the late 1990s, and aside from teaching my dogs to sit, down, and stay using dog treats as rewards from my teen years forward, this was only my second real training experience. But I learned. I got better over time. I finessed my game.

I'm going to confess something: I am glad I was a novice dog trainer when I started because it minimized how much I presumed about dog behavior. I had to pay more attention, and I had to learn to be a very good observer. Be like Zen Buddhists, who say, "First, empty your cup." Don't already know everything. Learn to observe like a raptor. Let yourself open up to what you're going to learn.

And fourth, while I do not recommend going over threshold on purpose, because it could backfire, in the instances when I went over threshold with some dogs, they still learned. They still became friends with me or with my dog. The procedure still worked. If you push and push the dog over threshold time and time again, you will fail. But if it happens accidentally once in a while, be prepared but know the dog is learning something of value. I'll teach you more about how to deal with going over threshold in the coming chapters.

As I've mentioned earlier, the reason we called our procedure Constructional Aggression Treatment was because of the work of Dr. Israel Goldiamond, who produced much excellent psychological research in the 1970s. Dr. Rosales admires his work very much, and he teaches all of his students to study Dr.

Goldiamond as well. Dr. Goldiamond's work involved setting up environments that made it as easy as possible for people to behave better. He then strengthened that better behavior by giving the learners something they liked. He called his work the Constructional Approach because the focus was on constructing, or building, new, preferred behaviors rather than punishing the problem behaviors. When we punish a behavior, we may get that behavior to go away, but there is always going to be another behavior that comes up to replace it. Rather than letting the dog decide on a behavior that creates another problem of its own either for us (maybe he now redirects his bites to his owner because biting the stranger got him in trouble) or for the dog (a life of stress in which, in his mind, he has to fear both his owner and the stranger), in CAT we specifically show the dog what behaviors are going to work. Turn your head? Yep, we'll make the scary stranger go away. Lunge? Nope, the scary stranger is going

The more you work with your dog, the more you will observe and learn about behavior.

to wait until you choose a better behavior—something we can reinforce—before going away. (Don't get started yet. We need to discuss lot more about the setup before you try this procedure.)

All organisms—dogs, sheep, people, cats, and so on— inherit the ability to adjust their behaviors in ways that make it more likely they will survive and have babies who will grow up and adjust their behaviors to survive, and so forth. Somewhere along the line, your dog's ancestors' aggressive responses to

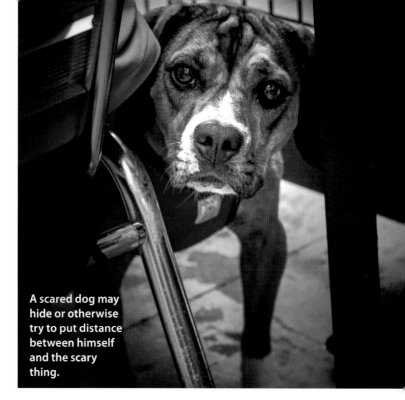

A scared dog may hide or otherwise try to put distance between himself and the scary thing.

threats preserved their lives and let them live on to breed and pass on their genes. What aggressive dogs want, however, is to perform behaviors that get immediate results; something they can see in the here and now. They probably don't have any concept of what their ancestors did to survive. They just want to do something that will make threatening things (people, animals, objects) go away or stop what they are doing at that moment.

Sometimes, in some situations, a dog will start trying to create distance between himself and whatever he doesn't like by trying to escape. But running away from a threat isn't always possible. Maybe the dog is on a leash, maybe he's in a fenced area, maybe he's in a kennel, or maybe a scary plumber has come into his home, and he can't get away. What then?

The dog does something that could chase the scary thing away. In no particular order, and possibly with other behaviors swapped in just because, he may freeze and carefully check out the situation. He may growl and then lower his head to get into position and then push off with his back legs, charge forward, and lunge. And maybe bite. These behaviors are scary as all get-out to most plumbers and other interlopers! They usually work, and they learn that this way of behaving almost always pays off. If it doesn't work one of these times, the dogs just aggress harder, eventually working up to full-on dangerous behavior. Such a dog is labeled "aggressive" by the people around him. Instead of being a dog who was just feeling threatened and wanting some relief, or who wanted to enjoy his own food in peace, he gets the moniker of "aggressive dog." And that's not good.

It's important to note that not all dogs want to chase scary things away. Sometimes a dog wants to interact (play) with someone, so he lunges and barks and leaps, and it looks like aggression. Barking and lunging don't always mean that the dog wants to hurt someone; sometimes a dog uses these behaviors to try to lure someone into interaction. The CAT treatment as explained in this book will not help these dogs who are are trying to interact socially but, for some reason, haven't learned to do it properly. What those dogs need are safe opportunities to learn how to play with other dogs. (Not the dog park! Dog parks are full of dogs with unknown behaviors and owners who pay more attention to their cell phones than their dogs.) It can be tricky to figure out the difference between "I want you to go away" and "I want to play with you" because sometimes what people call *play aggression* can look a whole lot like "I'm going to hurt you" aggression. And some playful dogs do end up hurting people because of their poor social skills.

Once I was called to perform the CAT procedure with a Rhodesian Ridgeback mix pup who was just less than a year old. His owners reported that he behaved aggressively around other dogs. I saw a video of his behavior, and it looked pretty fierce. I started to work on CAT with this dog, using my dear late Greyhound, Bravo, as my helper dog. She was a keen reader of dogs' body language, and I learned to trust her judgment. She was much better at reading dogs' body language than I will ever be. Bravo, for her part, didn't seem to find the puppy too worrisome from the very beginning.

We started to work, and I didn't feel as if we were getting anywhere. The closer Bravo and I got, the more crazed the pup seemed to get. I took a risk that I do not recommend for you unless you have a very strong fence between the aggressive dog and the helper dog. Normally, in the CAT procedure, when the dog behaves in a friendly (or somewhat less worrisome) way, the handler of the helper dog turns and walks away, taking the helper dog with her. (Remember, we're rewarding the dog with distance from the scary thing.) If the dog behaves aggressively, the handler waits until he calms down before walking away. (There is finesse to this, so don't start the work yet.)

In this case, I began to approach the Ridgeback with my Greyhound, bit by bit, doing the exact opposite of what we do in CAT with aggressive dogs. We moved closer when he acted better and walked away when he was aggressive, and what do you know? I quickly got close to the pup, and we found a nice, gentle pup who rolled over on his back as soon as my Greyhound got close enough to greet him. *This is the opposite of what we do with truly aggressive dogs and will not work with them!* The two of them sniffed, interacted, and were gentle and playful with each other. This pup wanted to play, but somewhere along the way, he had learned that barking and lunging were ways to get access to play. Or perhaps he was just frustrated that he never got to hang out with the dogs he was always being exposed to in training classes.

In another case, a Boxer would play roughly with his owner's boyfriend. The boyfriend would wrestle with the dog on the ground, grab his jowls, and engage in all kinds of roughhousing. Boxers are rough-and-tumble dogs who like to play hard, so this was fine with the dog, but it became a real problem for the girlfriend, who was the dog's owner. The unfortunate result of all this rough play was that the dog learned that barking, growling, lunging, and even mouthing with a hard pinch of the teeth were the ways to get someone to play. It wasn't long until his owner could barely handle him. It was quite a circus to teach the dog that rough stuff isn't fun for most people.

In this case, the couple broke up (I don't know if it had anything to do with the dog!). Having this guy out of the picture made it easier to eliminate the inappropriate play interactions. The usual routine was that the boyfriend would play with the dog, the dog would get too rough, and the boyfriend would punish the dog. The dog could have been left with no appropriate tools to solicit play. Fortunately, that wasn't the outcome for this Boxer, who learned how to play more appropriately with his mom, and his mom learned how to help him burn off energy with running and training activities rather than roughhousing.

This Boxer brings to mind something important. The build of the dog often affects his behavior because it affects what he is capable of and good at doing. A muscular breed (e.g., Boxer, Pit Bull, American and English Bulldogs, Bull

Terrier) is more likely to play by slamming and ramming into others. Why? Because their stout, muscular bodies bodies are very effective in controlling the behavior of other dogs and even people. If you watch two Pit Bulls playing in an appropriate way, you will likely see them run side-by-side and bump shoulders and hips while opening their mouths toward the other dog's face and mouth. Sooner or later, they may go tumbling head over heels with each other. This kind of dog play is not usually aggressive, and it is quite fun for them because they're built for it.

Put two Greyhounds together, and they're not likely to play this way. There are probably exceptions out there, but in general, that's not the Greyhound style. What are they going to do? They're going to run. They have deep chests with big, strong lungs, and they have powerful shoulders and hips to power their long,

thin legs. They have long toes to dig into the dirt and propel them forward. They don't usually ram into each other, at least not on purpose, and some of them will yelp like big, skinny babies (delightful big, skinny babies, I must say) if they have a

Digging is the next-best thing for many Jack Russell Terriers.

crash. Greyhounds have thin skin that tears somewhat easily, which is one of the reasons you often see racing or lure-coursing hounds wearing muzzles: to protect them from each other's teeth in case of accidental pileups. Animals, just like people, do more of what they can do well. Bully breeds slam; sighthounds run.

If you have a purebred dog, he may perform certain breed-specific behaviors because he is good at them. These behaviors have been selected by breeders for many generations over the lifetime of the breed. When dogs are bred for work, the ones who are the best workers are the ones that get to mate and produce babies. The dogs with the most susceptibility to reinforcement for the outcomes of the tasks they're supposed to perform get to pass their DNA on by breeding with other dogs who are also good at what they do. Border Collies herd. Jack Russell Terriers are vermin hunters and if there is no vermin they will figure out something else to do tenaciously if there are no vermin to hunt. Greyhounds chase rabbits and other critters that run (unless they are like Bravo, who was actually afraid of our cat, Mouse!)

If you have a mixed-breed dog, he may be susceptible to reinforcement for one of his ancestral breeds. One of my current dogs, Aero, who is part Afghan Hound and two parts herding dog (Australian Shepherd and Border Collie) finds the outcomes of herding reinforcing. But with many mixed breeds, you may not see anything that's necessarily breed-specific in their behavior. You will see dog-specific behavior as well as behavior resulting from the fact that they are living beings in the world. All organisms have the physical capacity to do things (such as creating distance) to avoid things they find aversive.

Choice is an important concern when working with the CAT procedure. In this procedure, we want to give the dog a lot of acceptable, effective choices. The fewer choices an animal has when faced with something aversive, the more likely he is to behave aggressively. If he can't run away because he's in a dog run or on a leash, he's more likely to behave aggressively. He's run out of choices, so to speak. One of the big challenges for dogs in our modern world is that they can't choose safe behaviors many times because they're trapped by the devices we use to keep them safe: leashes, crates, dog runs, fenced yards. I suspect this is one of the reasons there are more reports of aggression in dogs these days than when I was a kid in small-town Oklahoma, where dogs ran loose all day and were called in at night. If they saw a scary dog or person, heck, they could try to hide or outrun him. But now, dogs are contained so that they cannot run into traffic, dig up the neighbor's garden, get lost or stolen, and so forth. Their choices are all but gone. Since they can't choose to run, what are they supposed to do? They growl and show their teeth. I am not criticizing safety practices and laws regarding pets, but I do write this with some exasperation because I don't know the solution to keeping pets safe in a modern world while still providing them with full lives in which they can choose appropriate behaviors most of the time.

Often, a dog's aggression is orchestrated by us, his owners. Fifteen years before this writing, I adopted and brought home my little dog, Pan. He was about a year old at the time and weighed about 12 pounds. Of course, I thought he needed things, so I took him and Bravo off to the local pet-supply store. A child approached and asked if she could

it's rare for dogs to get to run free these days.

pet my dog, and before I could reply, she reached her hand out to Pan. He snapped. Oh, my! Fortunately, he did not make contact. I was mortified, but I had put my dog in over his head. I had only known him for one day. He had spent months with his brother in a shelter in eastern Texas, so why wouldn't he be wary of this impulsive small human in this wide-open space full of overwhelming sensory input without his brother for backup?

It was up to me to keep Pan from being overwhelmed, and I hadn't done it. Now, if the child had chosen to pet Bravo, it would have been a happy day for all because Bravo never saw a child she didn't adore, but Pan has always been happy to let other dogs be brave while he stands back and sounds the alarm. Pan didn't bite the child, and has never, to my knowledge, bitten anyone, but he did snap at that child as well as a couple of vets because he was in positions where he didn't have enough choices in his little doggy toolbox

to avoid behavior that could potentially stop their scariness in its tracks.

Interestingly and, obviously, in retrospect, when we switched to another vet in our town, Pan stopped snapping when he was examined. This vet was gentle and smooth, and he paced his exams to suit the little guy's comfort levels. One vet we saw would sit on the floor to examine my cat, Yoda, instead of putting him on the exam table. Yoda, who had previously needed to be sedated for exams, loved this vet. He rubbed on her and crawled into her lap as she palpated his belly, took his temperature, gazed into his eyes, and even when she opened his jaws to examine his teeth. Giving animals options they prefer often takes away their need to behave aggressively. If you are interested in finding a vet like this, check out the Fear Free Pets website at www.fearfreepets.com. Ask your vet if he or she is Fear Free-certified; if not, suggest that he or she pursues certification.

6

BE PERSISTENT AND CONSISTENT

> There is a huge difference between never permitting your dog to jump up on you, beg at the table, or join you on the couch and *almost* never allowing these behaviors to happen. The difference lets your dog question whether each occasion is one of the exceptions and keeps hope alive. It can make them seem quite pushy when they are really only unsure about what the rules are.
>
> ~Karen B. London, PhD

A man called me at the animal shelter. He was full of complaints about his dog and the trainer that I had sent to work with him. After each complaint, I explained carefully that the trainer was doing exactly what I would want her to do, and I tried to help him understand by reframing his complaints. He finally said, "You know what really bothered me? She seemed to be spending all her time trying to train me instead of the dog!"

Well, yes. Yes, I'm sure she did. She wanted to make sure that he knew how to handle the dog well, deal with problems as they arose, and resolve the intermittent issues he and his dog were having. He had to learn these skills, but he didn't pick up on the trainer's message. He thought she would come to his house and fix the dog's problems, and the duo would live happily ever after without having to change anything he was doing. It doesn't work that way. You have to change your behavior if you want your dog's behavior to change.

A major key to making this procedure work long-term is to commit to making sure that *your dog's* new behavior continues working for him. If you start doing this procedure only on occasion, you'll soon be complaining that CAT didn't work for your dog. No matter what training procedure or method you take up with your dog, you have to perform it consistently.

There are some tricky things that can happen if you train inconsistently. If you train new alternative behaviors to aggression very consistently, and you reinforce every time the dog performs a good behavior correctly, the dog is going to keep doing good things. If you never reinforce the good behavior again, it's going to stop happening. If you don't make the good behavior worthwhile, you will lose the good behavior.

To complicate matters, if the dog exhibits the desired behavior less frequently, he will find something else to do instead, and it will probably be the behavior you didn't like in the first place. After all, he already knows how to do that. So if you have taught your dog that sitting, turning his head, looking at you, or pulling the other way will result in your moving away from the neighbor on the street, but then you stop giving him his needed escape because you like to chat with neighbors on your walks, he's going to do something. The most likely thing for him to do is revert to his aggressive responses that worked so well in the past. *Hey, I'm on this leash, and this lady scares me. This new stuff Mom taught me isn't working, so I'm going to snap at the lady. That used to work every time.* You'll have wasted all that work, your dog could injure or anger your neighbor, and you'll have a lot more work to do to get back up to speed with your dog. This is true with CAT and every other training procedure that you or a trainer might do with your dog. In order to make the procedure work, you have to do the work.

There's a saying about insanity: "Insanity is doing the same thing you always did and expecting a different result." Well, doing the same thing and expecting a different result will not work with aggressive dogs, either. There are no quick tips a trainer can provide you over the phone that will resolve your aggression problem, although I get plenty of calls asking for just that. Your walks

This type of dog-park interaction can be overwhelming for many dogs.

will have to change during, and perhaps after, the training period, depending on how your training goes. If you want to chat with the folks in your neighborhood, you'll have to take your dog on a separate walk that is geared especially to his needs. If you just love going to the dog park, you'll have to go without your dog.

I once got a phone call from a woman inquiring about training for her dog who had suddenly become aggressive in the dog park after two big dogs attacked him. He had to get stitches. She then told me that ever since then, when she takes him to the dog park, he is mean to all the other dogs. There is a surefire solution to this: don't take that dog back to the dog park! Something bad happened to him there, and you likely can't do training sessions there because there will be a lot of off-leash dogs. So that's no longer where your dog needs to go.

If your dog bit the last repairperson who came to your house, you're going to have to work intensely on teaching your dog to enjoy spending time in his crate or in a room with the door closed with a rawhide or a food-stuffed toy while the worker is there. The worker doesn't have time to do a CAT session with you, and he or she probably has very little interest in working with aggressive dogs. If your dog has had problems with kids, and you have kids or kids who visit your home, you've got to teach both the kids and the dog some ways to deal with each other, and it's going to take time. The kids need to learn how and when to leave the dog alone, and the dog must be separated from the kids unless you're with them and paying close attention. I'm sorry. I know this is inconvenient. Having a dog with aggression is challenging.

Once you start doing CAT, make CAT a way of life. At first, it will be very intense, as will any aggression-resolution method you undertake, but it won't be as intense as living with uncontrolled aggression from your dog every day. Over time, you will find that your dog gets the idea and does the preferred behaviors more and more often while he performs aggressive behaviors less and less often. And if you go through the complete switchover process at the end of CAT (discussed later in the book), you will find that your dog will stop being so worried about strangers.

7

STARTING THE CAT PROCESS

So far, you've been doing your observation exercises and getting to know your pet and how he behaves in a variety of situations. Now read through the rest of the book without starting the work. This will give you a foundation for how you'll need to prepare and proceed. Starting with a solid read-through of the procedure will get you ready for when you start the work. At the same time, continue to observe your dog's behavior daily; it's very important that you know your dog's behavior well.

There are more questions in this chapter that you need to answer before you get started. Record all of the answers in your notebook or on your computer so that you can come back to it later. Without recording your process, it may be difficult to tell how much progress you're making; this is especially true during periods when progress is going slowly. There will be times when it seems as if you're not seeing improvement, but by checking your notes, you may see that more is happening than you realize. There may also be times when you seem to take a few steps backward. If this happens, or if you go several sessions without seeing improvement, it's time to step back and reevaluate what you're doing by rereading these procedural sections.

Each of the following questions is accompanied by how you will use the answer. That's where I will explain why the information is important. Answer these questions to the best of your ability, using experiences and observations you've had with your dog.

Does your dog have any health conditions?

How we will use this information: To determine if the heath condition could be affecting your dog's behavior.

When a dog doesn't feel well, he doesn't act like himself. Maybe he retains his good nature but is more reclusive or less active. Maybe he becomes irritable. Maybe he even growls and bites. As I mentioned previously, when my wonderful old Greyhound, Bravo, was eight years old, she became grouchy and started going off by herself to sleep in a different room, away from the family. One day, I bent down beside her to pet her, and she snapped at me. This was a behavior we had never seen before from that gentle old soul. A few days later, she stood up, and

her back leg broke. She had bone cancer and was in significant pain.

Visit your vet to make sure your dog is in good health before starting an aggression treatment. When I talked to one owner, who had a Red Heeler named Rudy, about taking her dog to the vet, it turned out that he had not seen a vet in nine years because he wouldn't allow even his owner to handle him that much. I suggested that she use a muzzle. She replied, "You can try it; I'm not going to." Uh oh. Nowadays, I would suggest that the owner find a vet who would prescribe medications to help Rudy through the process, including something that he could be given at home before coming to the clinic, or that she hire a mobile vet to come to her home, sedate Rudy,

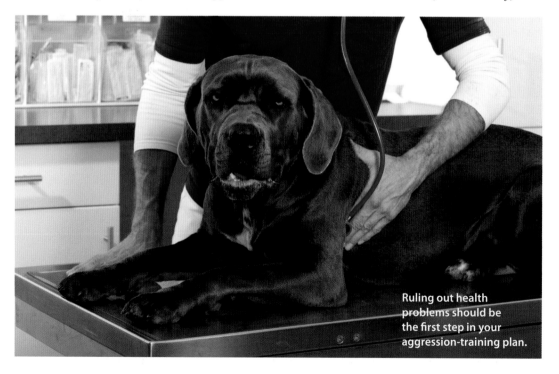

Ruling out health problems should be the first step in your aggression-training plan.

and examine him while he was sedated. There's no point in expecting a dog to tolerate more than he can actually tolerate. You can work on improving vet visits in a separate training project.

Rudy's eyeballs protruded in a bizarre fashion, and this trait was exaggerated when he barked. There are several health issues of varying severity that could have caused this, one of which is an untreated thyroid problem, which sometimes results in bulging eyes. Thyroid problems are sometimes associated with aggression and irritability in dogs. In spite of being unable to get a preliminary health workup for Rudy, an assistant and I worked with him for several sessions but made no progress. He had a long history of aggression, so he definitely needed behavioral support, but he also probably had at least one health issue that needed attention before a behavioral focus could be completely successful. Had he been able to visit the vet, we probably could have done more to

help him. Behavior doesn't get much better when the dog doesn't feel well.

Are your pet's health conditions believed to be related to his aggression? Why or why not?

How we will use this information: To determine whether we need to start or even complete medical treatment before starting behavior modification for aggression.

As I discussed about my dog, Bravo, and my client, Rudy, health problems can be related to the onset or the worsening of aggression. Even minor health issues can affect behavior. Are you in a good mood when you have a cold or a bellyache? Probably not. Sometimes identifying and resolving a dog's health issue is all is needed to eliminate the aggression; other times, the dog will need extensive treatment before starting behavioral training. The longer the behavior issue has been happening, the more likely you'll need to do some behavior modification before the aggression is completely resolved.

When did your dog first behave aggressively?

How we will use this information: The first instance of aggressive behavior may provide information about the behavior the dog is displaying now. It is important to note that we can still work with the dog even if we have no idea how the behavior began, but having this information can provide a helpful tool.

Sometimes, if we know what caused the first instance of aggressive behavior, it can help a great deal in the training. This is especially true if the aggressive behavior is relatively new. I worked for a while with a German Shepherd Dog who had

been "alpha rolled" (forcibly rolled onto his back and pinned down by someone in a misguided attempt for the person to establish dominance) as a four-month-old puppy. It is not unusual for alpha rolls and similar treatment to result in aggression from the dog. This kind of "training" is especially inappropriate for a puppy because it builds a foundation of fear and mistrust on which all of his future training experiences will be balanced. Because the young puppy was alpha rolled by a visitor to the home, the pup learned that strangers in his house are dangerous, which significantly impeded his family's ability to comfortably host gatherings in their home.

We used this information to decide where we would conduct our first training

The larger dog warns the smaller dog to back away from his bone.

sessions. We did them in the living room of the family's home.

How long ago was the first aggressive incident you observed?

How we will use this information: Knowing how long the dog has been behaving aggressively may inform us about how ingrained the aggressive behavior is.

If the dog has behaved aggressively for a short time, the first question is, "How is his health?" Sudden-onset aggression is often associated with something that just happened, like an injury or an acute illness. The next question is, "Have there been any changes in his life recently?" Has Grandma or a new roommate moved in? Is there a new family member, like a spouse, baby, or pet? Life changes, such as new members of the family, can set a dog off balance, as can moving to a new home, having work done in the house, or even just rearranging the furniture. Being attacked or growled at by a dog on a walk or being startled by a loud noise can make a dog wary.

How often does he behave aggressively?

How we will use this information: The frequency of the aggressive behavior can tell us whether the dog gets upset enough to lash out just occasionally or if it is his normal way of reacting to problems.

Sometimes owners will tell me that their dog is aggressive and they need help, but it turns out that he growled at another

Harsh treatment as a puppy can make a dog wary of people as he grows up.

family dog when he was six months old, another time when he was three years old, and then again last night when he was five. The rest of the time, the two dogs have been good friends. Sometimes dogs get grouchy, just like people do. When a dog displays aggression infrequently, we focus on anything out of the ordinary that may have been going on at those times. Was either dog sick? Was there a delicious treat in the area? Was one of the dogs guarding a favorite place or a favorite person? Was one of the dogs guarding an object that wasn't necessarily one of his favorite things just because he decided to guard?

There are times when one of these infrequent attacks is just too serious, and you'll need to manage the situation 100 percent of the time until you can work with a skilled positive-reinforcement trainer to resolve the behavior. If your dog has harmed a family pet or any human in the family, consult a trainer to help you set up safe management techniques and training in advance of working with your dog. Working with dogs who live together to resolve aggression issues is challenging. It requires that the dogs always be attentively supervised when they are together. It is very difficult to stay that tuned in all the time, so you must use safety equipment such as crates, baby gates, escape-proof exercise pens, and closed doors. These measures are not optional, and you must use them most of the time. Many dogs with interhousehold aggressive behaviors can never be loose in the presence of the other family pets.

Once you've identified when the aggressive behavior occurs, you must institute management right away. Feed treats only in separate rooms or in crates and remove the treats when the dogs are together. Feed meals the same way. Work on skills like "go to bed" and reward the dogs with a favorite treat instead of letting them get on the couch with you. Work on the very important skill "leave it," which means that the dog must drop an object or move away from whatever you're doing and pay attention. Use Exercise 3 from the observation exercises and take notes about what happened during a problematic interaction (obviously, you can't take notes until the incident is over and everyone is safe). What does your dog do just before he attacks the other dog? What does the other dog do just before he is attacked? How can you change the environment to make that situation less likely?

A dog who is aggressive toward other family pets poses additional challenges.

If you are having multiple incidences of aggressive behavior every day, starting a behavior program sooner rather than later is essential. You may even want to discuss medication with your veterinarian for the usual instigator dog as you start your behavior plan and then later work toward weaning him off the medication.

Consider how severe the attacks are. Behavioral treatments for severe bites and air snaps are very similar *except for the safety precautions taken*. If the dog has injured someone, anything from a red mark to a serious wound, you must take extreme safety measures. Because many factors can affect the outcome of a treatment, and because there is a risk of the behavior getting worse before it gets better, think long and hard about whether you are up for this. Remember, I cannot guarantee that you will be able to produce success with this procedure, and, for most of you, I cannot be there to oversee your work. Look in the mirror and decide if this is something you can safely undertake. Will working with this dog's aggression put you, the dog, your family and friends, your other pets, or your community at risk?

How many times has he behaved aggressively?

How we will use this information: To determine how common it is for your dog to resort to aggressive behavior.

Is your dog aggressive all the time, or did he behave aggressively for the first time yesterday? You are way ahead of the game if yesterday was the first time.

I love to hear from pet owners whose dog behaved aggressively and they're on the phone with me the next day. That means we can get to work and, in most cases, nip this in the bud quickly, whether you head to the vet for a complete workup or you start doing small CAT or management procedures right away.

Sometimes a pet owner waits to a call a trainer because he or she is not sure what to do or is avoiding dealing with what he or she fears may be a serious problem. The problem will most likely get worse if you delay behavior modification or other treatments. The longer the dog practices the behavior, and the more he falls back on aggression to solve his problems, the bigger the challenge will be.

Was the aggressive behavior reported to you by someone else, or did you see it yourself?

How we will use this information: To make sure that the behavior was accurately interpreted by the person who saw it.

If you didn't see it yourself, ask the questions you're answering now to the person who told you about the incident. In my work as a shelter behaviorist, I see and hear many reports about dogs' behavior. When I spend time with the dog myself, sometimes I see exactly what someone told me about, and other times I can tell that the person who reported it misinterpreted what they saw. People sometimes describe aggression with vague words like, "afraid," "dominant," and "alpha," or when they make assumptions like, "This dog must have been beaten by a man when he was small because he always tries to bite men." I prefer to go to the person who saw the behavior and ask about what he or she saw. What did the dog actually, physically do? Did he try to escape? Did he try to drive someone away? What actions did he take as he did that (e.g., ran behind the couch, lunged, barked)?

What does your dog do when he is behaving aggressively? Be specific. If you observed behaviors that seemed aggressive during your observations, go back to your notes and use that information to you help here.
How we will use this information: The behaviors that pose the greatest risk to the person or animal toward whom the dog behaves aggressively are the behaviors we want to reduce by replacing

them with preferred behaviors that are safe and friendly.

This is where you'll list behaviors like freezing, barking, growling, and lunging. Don't omit other behaviors you might observe, such as biting the leash, spinning in a circle, nipping the handler's clothes, turning, and trying to move away. We may use these behaviors during the CAT procedure.

Where does he behave aggressively now? List all or as many places as you can think of (inside the home, in the living room, on the couch, at agility class, at the park, on neighborhood sidewalks, in the backyard, and so on).
How we will use this information: These are the places where we will start doing the CAT procedure.

Ideally, you will start your dog's behavior modification in one of the places

Make specific notes about your dog's aggressive behavior and body language.

you identified. If you take the dog to work in a dog trainer's studio or an empty field because it will be easier to set up, it may work fine for the training session itself, but it may not help the dog understand that the same thing applies in the places and situations where he is currently having problems. It's OK to start working someplace other than where the aggression is happening, but afterward you will still have to move your training to the places where the aggression already occurs. It can be useful to practice setting up the work and working at a distance so the dog's reactions are minimal when you move to a different place.

What else is going on when he behaves aggressively? It could be anything: dinnertime, your arrival at home after work, someone ringing the doorbell, children playing, the dog chewing a rawhide that he doesn't want anyone else to get, and so on.
How we will use this information: This will be the activity we will set up when we conduct the CAT procedure.

Your answers to this question are very important in figuring out what makes him start to behave aggressively. When the scents of your delicious cooking start to waft through the home and the dogs gather around the kitchen, it may be more useful to crate them and give them treats for staying out of the kitchen rather than to launch a whole CAT training session. The goal of all of this work is to make it easy for your dog to do the right thing.

But if the behavior occurs because the dog finds value in chasing someone or something away, CAT is the way to go.

If the dog behaves aggressively when one of the owners arrives home, toward whom is the aggression directed? Is it toward the person who is coming home? Is it toward a person or animal who was already at home? If it's another pet, I very strongly suggest not leaving them loose together when you are not home.

What is the situation in which your dog's behavior causes you the most discomfort, concern, or inconvenience?
How we will use this information: This will give us the ideal place to start work.

The idea behind this question is to give you the greatest relief as soon as possible. We want to fix the most significant problem so you can have more peace in that situation.

Toward whom is your dog aggressive (adults, teenagers, children, dogs, a specific individual, an object, other)?
How we will use this information: To select helpers to work with us on the procedure.

The person (specific individual) or type of person (man, woman, man with beard, woman with hat) or animal or type of animal (cat, dog, hyena) toward whom your dog most often behaves aggressively must be involved in the procedure. Finding the right helper team can be one of the most difficult challenges in setting up any aggression treatment.

Sometimes the situations are so challenging that the treatment risk is greater than the potential benefit. If you're working with children, you can try starting out with dolls, but that will only get you so far. But let me be very clear: You must not use children to train your aggressive dog due to the very real potential risk to the child, whether emotional or physical. I do not recommend it, I discourage it, and I shudder to think about what could happen. Management using baby gates and doors, only allowing the dog out when the kids are not around, and tethering are possible, but conducting an aggression treatment with kids is truly tricky, and there is no guarantee that the dog will never behave aggressively toward them. Kids are impulsive. They get confused. They get scared. They misunderstand. They fall down suddenly and erupt into tears. A child's cries are just the thing to make others

uncomfortable, no matter how much we love children. Imagine how an anxious or bossy dog may respond.

If a child is at risk of being bitten by your dog, you really must consider whether the dog belongs in your family. Do you have children? Do children, including grandchildren, other relatives, and neighbors' children, ever come to your home? Do you plan to have children someday but already know that your dog behaves aggressively around children? Discussions with your family, pediatrician, and veterinarian may be in order.

Adults and some mature teenagers can be helpers during the training. You should explain the process to your helper, and he or she should agree to it and be completely cooperative. Ideally, he or she should read this book before you start.

If your dog is aggressive toward other dogs, you'll have to find an owner with a confident and friendly dog who will

As I've explained, the situations in which your dog is actually aggressive are the situations in which you need to work. If your dog behaves aggressively only while on a leash, you will have to train him on a leash. If he behaves aggressively only off leash, you must set up a situation in which he can be trained off leash. Often, a dog's aggression occurs primarily in the presence of one of the owners. For example, the dog may behave very well around the husband but may charge at other people when in the presence of the wife, or vice versa.

help you with the procedure. It's hard to find any person to work with your aggressive dog, but it's very, very hard to find someone who will expose his or her friendly dog to your aggressive dog. Explain that you will take every precaution for the dog's safety and that if there's any doubt or if his or her dog is overwhelmed, they can take a break or quit. Don't push the helper dog to the point that he is overwhelmed, or that dog may end up with problems similar to your dog's.

If your dog is aggressive toward both humans and dogs, the human handling the helper dog can be the first human you work your dog with. Two for the price of one!

Can you think of anything else related to when he is aggressive? For example, only when he's wearing a leash? When a certain person is around even though the aggression is not directed at that person? Other?
How we will use this information: To create more meaningful training setups.

I previously mentioned that I once worked with a Bull Terrier who was aggressive toward only one person, the wife's sister. The aggression occurred only when the husband was not at home. If the husband was anywhere at home—in the in the same room as the sister-in-law, the backyard, the bedroom, the garage—the dog was friendly toward her. But if the husband got in his car and drove away, the aggression began in earnest. This was very challenging to figure out, and I did it by testing different situations and recording everything carefully on video to review with Dr. Rosales. Once the wife told me that the dog had behaved aggressively toward her when she had borrowed her sister's perfume. That part was easy—I asked the sister-in-law and the dog's owner not to use that perfume anymore around the dog. I told you— behavior is interesting!

What do you or your family members currently do when the dog behaves aggressively? Does each family member respond to the aggression differently? Describe each person's reaction as thoroughly as possible.

What we will do with this information: Determine if the family members need to change their behavior as part of their lives with the dog going forward. Trust me, you will need to make changes.

Often, families respond impulsively to aggression from their dogs. The dog lunges, and the owner may yell or swat or forcibly pull the dog away by the collar. If you have responded in this knee-jerk way, you are not alone. It has happened to me, too. But now that we know these types of reactions are not helping the situation with the dog, we will use this information to teach you some alternative responses that will help reduce the likelihood that your dog will behave aggressively. Stay tuned.

Sometimes, owners comfort their dog after he behaves aggressively. The owners understand that their dog is upset, and they love their dog, so they want to calm him. The motivation is good, but the outcome can be a problem; in some cases, it can result in the unwanted effect of strengthening the aggression. I remember an owner leaning over her large dog, who had just lunged at me, and saying, "Oh, baby, it's OK!" Well, it wasn't OK! It wasn't the right time to be rewarding the dog's behavior. Yes, the dog was upset, and we definitely don't want to keep the dog in a place of emotional turmoil. But we needed to reset the situation. In this case, the ideal would have been for me to wait for the dog to do something else besides aggressing and then, when that happened, for me to walk away, and then the owner could interact with her dog.

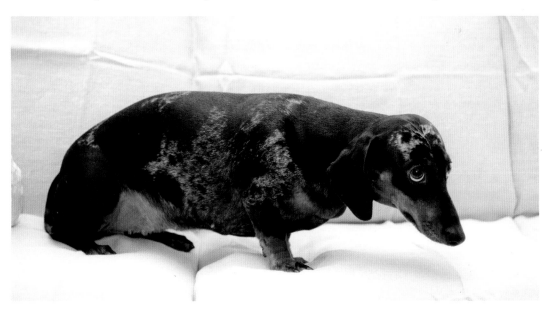

If you're in a situation where your dog is aggressive toward someone who either doesn't know what to do or can't be expected to cooperate (e.g., someone walking in the neighborhood), walk the dog away or, if possible, get him to respond to a cue. Then reward him. Don't reward him immediately after an act of aggression for two primary reasons. One, as I've said, is the risk of rewarding and thus reinforcing inappropriate and potentially dangerous behavior and seeing it happen more often in the future. The other is the risk of the dog not being done with his aggressive episode yet and redirecting his aggression onto you. Take a deep breath, walk the dog away until he's far enough

from the situation that he can calm down, cue an easy behavior, and then reward with a treat. Help him switch gears.

Are there any situations or times during which the dog is not aggressive? What are they?

How we will use this information: To indicate that the dog has the ability to behave in nonaggressive ways and to identify in what situations he behaves nonaggressively.

The dog's nonaggressive behaviors are going to help us build toward our goal. Maybe we know that the dog is wiggly around his owner but growly around the owner's boyfriend. We know that one of his

This dog is showing signs of stress from being hugged. The exaggerated wrinkles above the eyes, the closed mouth, and the staring eyes all point to the dog's feeling uncomfortable.

happy behaviors is wiggling, so we want to reward more and more wiggly behavior in the presence of the boyfriend, a little tiny bit at a time.

No dog is aggressive 100 percent of the time. Sometimes they are asleep, for example. You probably wouldn't have this dog if he wasn't friendly with you at least some of the time. Aggression is situation-specific. The answers to this question will help us trust that our dog is able to behave in friendly ways. And it will help us know what to look for as we start to shape appropriate behavior to replace aggression in your dog.

What does your dog do when he is not behaving aggressively?

How we will use this information: To identify what behaviors to reward as we conduct the CAT procedure.

Your dog does something you like, and we want to make it easy for him to do more of that behavior in more situations. This question will help us focus on the goal.

What previous training, if any, has your dog had? To be clear, I'm talking about intentional training, such as classes, private consultations with trainers, or sessions with a trainer in which you focused on teaching new behaviors or discontinuing problematic behaviors.

How we will use this information: Each training experience has had some effect on your dog, some more than others. Your dog learns different things from different kinds of training. This section

will help us understand what kinds of training you, as the handler, and your dog will have to strengthen or undo to be successful going forward.

How many trainers, if any, have you worked with for aggression? Each trainer you've worked with may have done different things to teach your dog that different behaviors will result in different outcomes. It is particularly important to understand is that sometimes aggression-rehabilitation techniques teach a dog to shut down and simply not respond. This happens with shock collars as well as with some desensitization techniques and even with some positive reinforcement. The problem is that some dogs shut down only until their threatening person or animal gets close enough that they can attack. Remember, in the CAT procedure, we want to reinforce movement because the more the dog moves, the more we have to work with and reward. If we reinforce being still, it's much harder to tell what the dog is going to do next.

When did you work with the trainer and for how long? This question simply identifies how much practice this dog has experienced with this technique.

If your dog was a four month old puppy that was introduced to a shock collar after an instance of reactivity, and he is now four years old and behaving aggressively, this is a dog that got a really potent lesson from that shock at a very sensitive time in his life. At four months old, most puppies have a relatively small number of life experiences to draw from. Now being shocked is part of the foundation of all future learning. It's easy for a four-month-old puppy to learn that strangers are dangerous, and because they don't have much in their behavioral repertoires to draw from, they fall back on that information they got as a puppy. For this dog, we're going to have to repair his foundation. The longer he's balanced his behavioral weight on this foundation and the more behaviors he has learned while relying on that information, the more work will need to be done to rehabilitate his behavior.

What did this trainer do with your dog or recommend that you do with your dog? Did you act on these recommendations, and for how long? How did your dog respond? Was the goal of the training to teach the dog that there were many things he could do to get a worthwhile outcome in the face of a threat? Or was the goal just for the dog not to respond aggressively?

When a dog learns not to do something in a certain kind of situation, another behavior has to take its place. If your dog was taught not to do anything, the dog actually did learn to do something. It was just something that was much harder to see and work with.

What is your evaluation of the training outcome? Did the trainer or your previous attempts at resolving aggression work to improve the aggression? Did the aggression get worse? Did it stay about the same? What changes would you like to see that didn't happen? What changes happened that worked well for you and your dog?

Has your dog been under a veterinarian's care or treatment for aggression?

How we will use this information: We need to know if the dog is already under medical care for health concerns related to aggression or for aggressive behavior alone, what the vet has recommended, and how you have followed up. It's important for us to know if the treatment helped.

Has the dog been on medication for aggression? Some medications will moderate the dog's responses to a threat, and that is, in a sense, what they are intended to do. The goal is to reduce the inappropriate responses and reduce the emotionality of the responses. You can start the CAT procedure with a dog who is taking medication, and, as

How much
training
in basic
behaviors
has your
dog had?

the treatment proceeds, you and your vet can determine if he can be weaned off of the medication. Do not start your dog on medication and then abruptly stop it without the advice and guidance of your veterinarian. Sometimes withdrawal symptoms can be bad.

What medication(s) is/was your dog on (if any)? Let me stress that I am not a veterinarian. I cannot prescribe medications nor can I make your vet unprescribe them. But I can tell you some things you can research further for yourself. Some medications are quite suitable for working with dogs with stress and aggression. Others are not. Acepromazine is one of the medications your dog should *not* be taking for aggression, but some veterinarians still prescribe it. This medication will reduce the dog's behavioral responses, but his emotional responses will not

change. It is sometimes referred to as a "chemical straitjacket." Performing a behavior-modification procedure on a dog who is taking acepromazine is likely to be counterproductive, so if your dog is taking this medication, tell your vet that you would like to switch to one of the antidepressant or antianxiety medications or withdraw him from the medication completely. If your veterinarian is not experienced in the use of these medications or refuses to work with you, get a second opinion from a different vet. Likewise, if your vet is not on board with discontinuing acepromazine, get a second opinion.

Check the list of vets on FearFreePets. com to find one in your area. These vets have training in the use of the most appropriate drugs for behavior problems. As I said earlier in the book, do consider giving your dog medication to help him through this problem, but make sure you have good information to help you decide.

When and for how long was your dog on medication? Was the medication something intended to help him through a rough patch? If he no longer takes the medication, why?

Is your dog still taking medication? If yes, why? Is it helping? If not, discuss alternatives with your vet or get a second opinion.

What is your evaluation of the outcome of past or current medications? If the medication is not having the desired

effect, talk to your veterinarian about weaning him from the medication. If the medication is working, how is it working? Does the dog react better in the situations in which he was previously aggressive? Define *better*. What do you consider a success? If the medication is helping, and your veterinarian agrees, there is no reason to remove the dog from the medication to start the CAT treatment. In most cases, medical treatment is enhanced by appropriate nonaversive behavioral treatment.

Did the veterinarian prescribe nonmedical treatment for aggression?

How we will use this information: Your veterinarian is an expert on veterinary medicine, but only some veterinarians also have expertise in animal behavior. The answers to this group of questions will help you determine whether you will follow your veterinarian's nonmedical behavioral advice.

Does your veterinarian have training in animal behavior? Many veterinarians are exposed to some behavioral information in their training, often associated with the use of pharmaceuticals to ameliorate emotional problems. Ask your vet what kind of behavioral training he or she has had. Is he or she a certified member of the American College of Certified Veterinary Behaviorists? If not, how much ongoing training does he or she receive in behavior, and where does he or she receive it? If your vet's response is that he or she gets enough behavior information just by working with animals every day, keep in mind that the work that most vets do is likely focused on medical concerns rather than behavioral concerns. Often, vets and vet techs know how to get through a procedure but not how to help the dog tolerate the procedure. If you can find a Fear Free-certified veterinarian, this vet may provide very good support for the work you're about to do with your dog.

Did you follow the vet's recommendations? If you not, why? Was it too difficult or time-consuming? Did it seem too harsh? Were the results too slow? Was it complicated? Did you suspect it would be counterproductive?

What did the intervention involve? Did the technique help your dog learn a wide array of alternatives to aggression, or did it try to shut down behavioral responses? Was it a system of management, such as containing dogs away from guests with doors and baby gates or crates? As we have discussed, the goal should be to build alternative responses to aggression that are as easy as possible for the dog to perform. If it's hard for the dog to do the right thing, he's not going to do it. Likewise, if it's hard for you to do the things you're instructed to do, you're less likely to do them.

Did the veterinarian's recommendation work? Did your dog behave aggressively less often, or did his aggression become milder? If you did follow the recommendation, and it produced results that improved your life and the life of your dog, maybe you should just stick with that program. If you followed the recommendation but felt that the results were not good enough, discuss the shortcomings of the treatment with your vet. Tell your vet where you felt the method fell short and ask if there are ways to make it more effective. Ask if there are adjustments you can make to improve the outcome. Also, before discontinuing the treatment, make sure that you have been following the protocol as closely as possible.

As with trainers, if your vet recommends aversive tools (shock collars, prong collars, pinning your dog down, or shouting into his face, for example), don't do it. Find another vet.

What kind(s) of handling gear (leash, flat collar, slip or choke collar/chain, electronic collar, prong collar, body harness, head halter, other) do you use with your dog?

How we will use this information: To identify safe and effective gear to use during the CAT procedure and gear that is appropriate for you to use after CAT.

There are some kinds of gear that are inappropriate for use with the CAT training procedure, including (but not limited to) slip chains and leads, prong collars, shock collars, bark collars, and flexible (retractable) leads. In fact, these tools are not appropriate in most situations. Any gear that works by causing pain or discomfort could very well teach the dog that every time he sees something he considers threatening (a dog, a person,

FENCE ME IN

Replace invisible fences (fences that shock the dog when he crosses a certain point) with physical barrier fences, like chain-link or privacy fences, before you begin CAT training. The aggressive dog needs a complete reset. Your goal is to convince him that the world is not completely crazy and dangerous so that he can settle down and behave in confident and friendly ways.

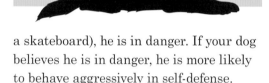

a skateboard), he is in danger. If your dog believes he is in danger, he is more likely to behave aggressively in self-defense.

The goal of CAT is to help your dog be less afraid or defensive in the world he lives in. The goal of harsh training tools is to increase his discomfort to force him to stop behaving aggressively. However, this is not how to end aggression. These tools just drive aggressive behaviors underground to make your dog's behavior sneakier and less predictable. If you use any of these tools, you must discontinue their use once you start the CAT procedure, including between and after CAT training sessions. You can't switch back and forth between CAT and aversive training techniques and find success.

There are other types of collars that don't normally cause physical pain or discomfort but are annoying or troubling to the dog in other ways; these include citronella collars and collars that blow a

burst of air into the dog's face. We don't want to convince your dog that the things that threaten him are also annoying. We want to teach him that they aren't a problem.

Head halters can be useful tools for some dogs, but, unfortunately, I have seen dogs with aggression lunge into them during aggressive episodes, and I am very concerned about an injury happening to a dog's neck. Another trainer told me about seeing a large dog lunge aggressively into a head halter and injure his neck severely, causing a loss of balance for several months. For this reason, I discourage the use of a head halter during CAT training. In addition, unless your dog is trained to make a positive association with the head halter prior to CAT, you could have a dog who is so focused on the weird thing on his head that he can't learn anything you're trying to teach him about aggression. He's also likely to associate this new equipment with the procedure, and he may avoid training sessions by hiding or transferring his aggression to the person applying the head halter. If your dog is already accustomed to wearing a head collar and doesn't seem to notice when he's wearing it, you can continue to use it, but attach your training leash to the collar or body harness so that there is less risk of injury if he lunges forward.

Muzzles are excellent safety tools that may protect your dog from the quarantine and possible euthanasia that can result from a bite, and they can protect your

Left: If you will use a body harness, accustom your dog to the harness before CAT training begins.

Below: Make sure your dog is accustomed to the training gear you will use before you start training.

helpers by preventing bites. Just like with the head halter, you should train your dog to wear a muzzle before you start CAT training. There is an excellent video called "Teaching Your Dog to Wear a Muzzle" by trainer Chirag Patel on YouTube about how to do it. If you are concerned about your dog biting you, work with a positive-reinforcement trainer to teach him to wear the muzzle safely. You should wear protective gloves during this process just in case.

Has anyone recommended euthanasia for your dog because of his aggression, or have you considered it on your own?
How we will use this information: To determine if this recommendation is valid.

If someone has suggested that your dog be euthanized, we need to determine whether his or her point is valid. Is your dog a danger to anyone? Does someone in your family have an extreme fear of dogs that he or she needs professional help with? (I've worked with family members who were afraid of the family dog and didn't want to come home because the dog was there.) Is the person or animal toward whom your dog behaves aggressively doing something that makes the dog behave aggressively? Or is this person overreacting? Sometimes a family member who does not live with the aggressive dog is irritated or scared, or the person's feelings are hurt by the dog's behavior, which may cause the person to mention euthanasia. In this case, you need to educate the family member. Let him or her know that you are working with the dog and tell the person about the training, as well as the safety precautions you are taking, to make living with the dog safer. Be humble and show your concern rather than being defensive. Can you visit this person at his or her home instead of having him or her come to your home during the course of the dog's training? Can you crate the dog in a separate room during visits? The latter point will require the person to never walk into your home unannounced so that you have time to crate the dog.

If the person is recommending euthanasia because your dog injured someone, how bad was the injury? Did the person need medical care? Was the dog quarantined or labeled an aggressive dog by the municipality you live in? Is there a chance of legal problems with this person? How can you prevent this from happening again? Will a lock on the gate solve the problem? Answer all of these questions after careful thought. Be honest with yourself.

Using a chain choke collar or any other aversive training tool risks worsening a dog's aggressive tendencies.

If the person provided a reason for his or her euthanasia recommendation, what was it? Was the recommendation reasonable? Is it something you need to seriously consider?

If you're reading this book because you still have the dog and still want to work with him, why did you keep him? Is he your best friend? Or is it because you'll never let your mean neighbor win an argument? Honestly. What is the likelihood that you can follow through this process of CAT training safely?

Has anyone recommended rehoming your dog because of his aggression, or have you considered it on your own?

How we will use this information: To determine whether your dog can safely remain in your home and whether you realistically think there may be a home out there where the dog will not hurt anyone.

Who recommended rehoming? Was it a family member, friend, veterinarian, or trainer? Or was it your idea? Sometimes a person will recommend rehoming because he or she can see that your dog is not a complete danger in every situation, but he or she doesn't think the dog's a good fit in your family. Maybe your dog has knocked down your elderly live-in mother and there's a risk of him injuring her. Maybe your dog is not nice to the friends your children bring home, and their parents are concerned about it.

Management is an option but, as dog trainers say, "Management always fails."

A child or worker will leave a gate open. A close friend will walk right into your house without giving you time to crate your dog. You'll be carrying groceries and unable to put him in his safe space in time. These things can happen; because we're human, sometimes we'll make mistakes. Consider this when deciding if your dog can stay in your home.

If the person provided a reason for the recommendation, what was it? Was the recommendation reasonable? Is it something you need to seriously consider? This is the time for serious reflection.

If you didn't rehome him, why not? Are you ready and able to move forward with life with a reactive or aggressive dog? It is very difficult to find a new home for

a dog with aggression problems. If you still have your dog because you simply can't find someone else to take him, you may need to revisit the euthanasia question. But if you are truly committed to your dog, and you truly are committed to doing everything necessary to keep everyone safe, and you understand the responsibility you're undertaking, CAT, combined with management, might be a solution for you.

What does your dog do that you value (appearance, breed, tricks, canine sports, companion, sad story at the shelter, and so on)?

How we will use this information: To stress the bond between you and your dog.

Why do you love your dog? Now is the time to ask yourself this question. Do you love your dog? What made you get him in the first place? Was that reason a good reason to adopt this dog? When you look at him, what do you feel when he looks at you? Is that feeling an indication of how well you will be able to conduct the CAT procedure successfully?

Why else do you value him? What has happened since you got your dog that has made you keep him this long? Some people report a genuine love for their canine companions. Others hint at guilt over not being able to keep their dogs.

Do you feel that your dog's aggression limits your life? How?

How we will use this information: To help determine if your dog's presence in your life is worth the sacrifices you make for him. Sometimes the impact on a family's life is so profound that keeping a dog with aggression can severely affect the quality of life for both the animal and the people in the family.

These ideas feel harsh, I know, but the fact is that we all make sacrifices for our dogs. Beyond food, shelter, and veterinary expenses, we have to clean up their messes when they are puppies and again when they are old and occasionally in between. If they develop aggression, we may have social messes to clean up as well. One owner of a large aggressive dog told me that she had decided that it was worth it to her not to date for the anticipated life span of her dog, another ten years, because her dog would not let men into her home. Is that you? Are you willing to do whatever it takes? Or are you like the young parents of a one-year-old child whose dog had begun to growl at the child when she began to walk? They worked on training and a variety of techniques for managing their child and their dog, but ultimately they decided they couldn't safely sustain these efforts. Those parents truly loved their dog, but they could not live with the risk to their child's safety. They were able to find an adult home where the large mixed-breed dog would not have to live with a clumsy, impulsive toddler who put him far outside his comfort zone.

List all the things you would do with your dog if he didn't have aggression.

How we will use this information: To start building socially acceptable behaviors that will let you do those things with him. Maybe you just want your dad to be able to come over and visit without crating your dog the entire time. If your dad will participate in the training, it's possible that this could happen. Maybe you want to be able to walk with your dog in the park. Along with being proactive to prevent others from making it too hard for him, the CAT procedure may help you do this, too.

The fact of the matter is that there are things I do not recommend doing with an aggressive dog. Many families enjoy going to dog parks, for example, but their dogs don't. One family I talked with had a dog who had been attacked by two large dogs in a dog park and thereafter began to behave aggressively toward dogs. When I recommended that they stop taking their dog to dog parks, they were surprised. The woman asked, "Really?" in a bewildered voice, followed by a long silence. Yes, really. Dog parks are full of all kinds of dogs, some with various behavior problems. Sometimes a perfectly nice dog will be a brat when he's around his posse and will pick on another dog. If your dog has aggression issues, off-leash dog parks, where dogs are running amok and owners are usually either chatting with each other or looking at their phones and not paying attention to their dogs, are not ideal environments. All of these factors can be a recipe for replacing the desirable behaviors you just built with those old aggressive behaviors. Often, even if an owner is paying attention to his or her dog in the dog park, he or she may not understand what is happening between the dogs. I can tell you many stories about people who thought that the dogs were being playful just before they bit.

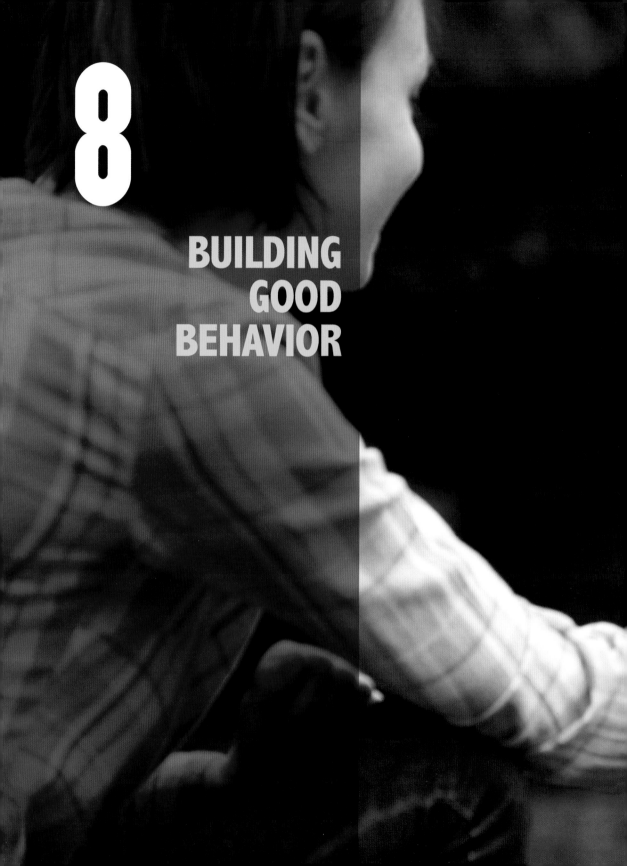

8

BUILDING GOOD BEHAVIOR

> **Sometimes a dog doesn't want a treat. Sometimes he wants relief.**

The Constructional Aggression Treatment is not designed to force the bad behavior out of an aggressive dog's bag of tricks. Usually, when dog owners are asked what they want their aggressive dog to do, they say "I want him to stop being aggressive!" If this is how we approached stopping aggressive behavior, we would have to punish the dog harshly while he was exhibiting aggressive behavior, using such good timing that the dog would know that behaving that way was a bad idea. Effective punishment (or correction) reduces the frequency of the behavior or stops the behavior from happening in the future. This sounds good on the surface, but as I wrote in the chapter on punishment, there are all kinds of problems that come along for the ride.

One of the problems is simple: What is the dog going to do instead of the aggressive behavior? A dog can't just stop doing everything. If he stops behaving aggressively, he has to do something else instead. Some dogs are taught to just be still, which often makes them more dangerous. Still dogs have been known to suddenly snap—or worse—if you get too close. If we teach them not to growl, they'll pick something else, such as a lunge. Such as a bite. Such as urinating and cowering under the bed. These aren't the kinds of solutions most people want for their dogs' aggression, but there's plenty of research to demonstrate this kind of behavioral response. I hear stories all the time about how dogs respond to punishment.

I got a phone call from a woman who had called me five months earlier because her dog, Brutus, had behaved aggressively, and she was looking for some help. The first time she called, I talked to her for quite a while and urged her to make an appointment for a private behavior consultation in her home so that our trainer could see what was going on and help the family set up some management and figure out how they were going to move forward because—guess what? The woman had found out she was pregnant the day after her dog bit her. She was convinced the dog had figured out she was pregnant. I was not successful in convincing her that it was unlikely that her pregnancy caused the aggression.

Unfortunately, she did not make an appointment. Instead, she watched all the videos she could find of a TV dog trainer. The methods involved pinning the dog to the floor when he growled, showing him who was the pack leader when he wouldn't get into his bed by physically forcing him onto his bed and holding him there, or kicking his backside when he refused to go into his crate. Brutus complied when they first started these tactics, sometimes with a growl that got him an extra kick or scolding. But here's the deal: The dog was a purebred adult male American Bulldog who weighed 90 pounds. He was pure muscle; a powerful dog. When the owner called me the second time, it was because he had bitten her while she was straddling him and teasing him. He'd decided that he'd had enough. His owner said, "We won't tolerate a dog who will do this." But what was the dog supposed to do? He had tried to tell them. He had tried to tell them that he was at the end of his rope.

Brutus's last bite landed on the grandma-to-be, who kept messing with his jowls even after he tried to move away

The crate is a helpful tool that should never be used as punishment.

from her and even after he growled at her to emphasize how uncomfortable he was. When she kept messing with him, he finally bit her. Can you blame him? To the poor dog's credit, he only injured her arm; it could have been much worse.

So the family had an intact (unneutered) American Bulldog who had only been trained with force and who was often as friendly as he could be. He had been expected to put up with unfair, escalating teasing even after he tried to get away, and even after he growled. He had finally bitten at least two people, and now a new baby was only a few weeks away. What a recipe for disaster. The owners asked if I could teach them how to teach the as-yet-unborn baby to be dominant over the dog. Yet they couldn't manage him as adults. The family fortunately determined that they could not keep the dog because "a dog will understand who is boss in our family; that is not optional." It's also not realistic if the dog receives unfair treatment and doesn't have his needs considered.

There are different kinds of leaders. At one end of the spectrum, you have an uneducated and impulsive boss who isn't really a leader at all. He or she is just a bully. This person doesn't give clear information about his or her expectations for the dog's performance and berates the dog, threatens him if he doesn't comply, and is generous with punishment. Play is one-sided and may consist of teasing by adults or mistreatment by children who aren't taught to respect animals. At the other end is a true, benevolent leader who makes it easy for the dog to understand what to do and who looks for opportunities to reward the dog for improvements. Even before the dog knows how to do what this leader wants, the leader starts showing him what parts of it he did almost right, what parts he's improving on, and how he can get what he needs from his world. This is done by providing reinforcement on every occasion possible. This benevolent leader figures out what the dog values so that he or she can reward the dog in a way that motivates him to cooperate with the training process and the leader.

Which kind of leader do you need to be to help your dog? Obvious, isn't it? In this process, you are not going to be surprised if the dog can't read your mind about what to do instead of aggressing. You're going to get creative about figuring out ways to help him understand. The behaviors

Physical reprimands, such as grabbing the dog by the scruff of his neck, do nothing to improve—and usually worsen—a dog's behavior.

Once you know why your dog is behaving aggressively, you can begin to help him.

you're going to help your dog learn must work just as well for him as the aggression did in providing distance from things he can't deal with very well. Ideally, the new behavior will be something he cannot do at the same time as aggressive behavior. For example, a dog who is wiggling and grinning can't bite very well, so we want to help your dog feel like wiggling and grinning. We're not going to take away one behavior and then let him figure out other things to do on his own. He might not make the right choices. We're going to show him how to succeed.

Your dog has been showing you what he wants as a reward for his aggressive behavior all this time. He wants others to leave him alone or stop what they're doing. Your aggressive dog already knows how to make other people go away and leave him alone or how to make them knock off the nonsense. Do you think that Brutus's

grandma didn't back off (finally!) when he bit her? He tried to tell her that he'd had enough when he walked away from her. It didn't work. He tried to tell her that he was over his limit when he growled. It didn't work. But when he bit her, she finally got the message. So what did Brutus learn? Walking away doesn't make people leave me alone. Growling doesn't work, either. Biting works.

Distance from annoyances, threats, and fearsome things is what the aggressive dog usually wants. In the CAT procedure, we are not going to force a dog go into his crate by kicking him. We're not going to demand that he endure more than he is already telling us he can endure just because we're supposed to be the leaders. Instead, we're going to pay attention to what he's trying to tell us and help him learn new behaviors that will help him be more successful in his life with humans.

How do we do this? The first thing we need to do is figure out what he is trying to accomplish with his aggression. What does he get out of it? Does he bark and growl to get people or dogs to come closer like the Ridgeback mix I described earlier who was frustrated because he never got to play? CAT isn't the right treatment for that dog. Or does he want people or dogs to go away and keeps behaving aggressively because he knows that it works to make them go away?

What does Brutus want? He wants to get people to get out of his face because so many people have used force with him and ignored his attempts to tell them he was in over his head. He had learned that his initial safe choices of moving away and even growling were not effective deterrents to unwanted physical manipulations of his body. He had learned that he had to bite if he wanted people to knock it off. The owner told me that it seemed as if he didn't like to be told what to do. It sure sounds that way. It sounds like he was most often expected to do things that were very unpleasant for him. What if they had tried rewarding good behavior and making it easy for him to understand what good behavior was?

If you have used forceful methods with your dog,

it doesn't make you a bad person. Correction-based training has been with us for a long time and doesn't seem ready to die out in the United States anytime soon, although some other countries are stricter about the treatment of animals. With the Internet full of different handling methods and training techniques, it's hard to know what's best. But if you've tried certain techniques and your dog has become worse, or he is fine until he's close enough to bite, or he has shut down and lost his interest in being engaged with the world, let's start over and try something different. Clean slate.

As I've mentioned repeatedly so far, our goal is to teach your dog new behaviors that he can do instead of behaving

Positive training is a partnership between owner and dog.

Identify the situation(s) in which your dog's aggression occurs.

aggressively. How do we do that? The first thing we need to think about is where the aggression takes place. Aggression is situation-specific. There are situations in which it happens and situations in which it doesn't. *Situation* is a pretty generic word, so let me illustrate what I mean.

Riley was not aggressive toward me on the sidewalk in front of his house, at the front door, or even in the backyard. Those situations were not problems. But he lunged and barked at me as I was entering the living room. That situation was a problem. So our work had to begin upon entering the living room.

Sabrina was only aggressive toward her female owner's sister and only at their home but not when her male owner was anywhere in the home or on the property. So, part of the situation was the presence of the owner's sister at their home. In addition, she was only aggressive if the male owner got in his car and drove away.

So her situation also involved the absence of the male owner. Her work had to be done with the sister present in the home and the male owner absent.

There are some dogs who behave aggressively around food, and others who protect the couch or the bed. There are certainly mother dogs who will protect their puppies. You may hear these behaviors referred to as different types of aggression, but really these are the situations in which aggression occurs. If your dog's aggression never occurs in the park, you do not have to work in the park, although it won't hurt if you do. If the aggression happens only in your front yard, that is the only place you need to work. Many dogs behave aggressively in more than one situation, so figure out which situation has the most significant impact on your life and start there. You will need to work in multiple situations if your dog behaves aggressively in multiple situations.

Part of the situation is the people who are around when aggression occurs, both the person toward whom your dog behaves aggressively and the person holding his leash or standing nearby. If the dog behaves aggressively toward one specific person, that person will have to be involved in the training. If the dog behaves aggressively toward a category of people, such as men or, even more specifically, men with beards, you'll start with a bearded guy as your helper and then do the work with other bearded guys, again and again, until your dog gets the idea that the world works the same way no matter what guy it is.

You may find that the human holding the leash can affect whether a dog behaves aggressively. As I mentioned, I was working with a Greyhound who behaved aggressively toward guests in her living room. The wife worked with me, holding the leash, and I acted as the interloper since I was a stranger to the dog. After a while, we had made a lot of progress with me entering the home, and the dog's aggression was getting much less intense. Then the husband walked through the room. She lost it and began to aggress vigorously, so we had to work a lot more with the husband.

I worked with a small terrier who behaved aggressively to pretty much anyone she didn't know, but only if her owner wasn't around. If her owner was holding her leash, she acted fine. This

made it quite tricky to leave her with friends or a house sitter when the owner traveled. So we worked with strangers holding her leash and with strangers approaching her while her leash was held by someone other than her owner.

If you're having trouble figuring out the situations that affect your dog's aggression, consider these points: Is it in the morning or evening? Is it cold or hot outside? Do you hear any sounds when it is happening? (With sounds, if you can make the sound stop, you may not have to do anything else.) Does it happen when children are playing noisily in the house? (Making this the dog's crate time away from the kids could be the right management solution.) Is it immediately after you arrive home from work? (Until you do further treatment, can you make homecomings less exciting? Or keep the dog in a different room so he can't approach the front door until he's calm?)

You are most likely familiar with using treats to reward behavior you like. In CAT, instead of using treats as rewards, you are going to reinforce the behavior you like by removing something (person or animal) that the dog doesn't like. To make this as minimally aversive as possible, start working with your dog far enough away from the other person or animal that he doesn't get very worried. Set up a safe training environment in a space that is significant to the dog's aggression (in other words, in a place where the aggression often occurs) and then introduce the threatening person or dog. (I'll talk about

how to select these helpers in the coming chapters. These will be helpers we can instruct to behave in certain ways as we create a controlled training environment for the first stages of the work). The goal is to keep the "threat" (a.k.a. the helper) far enough away from the dog that the dog doesn't get worked up about it. Ideally, we'll be far enough away that the dog notices the threat but doesn't respond to it much at all.

For some dogs, the threat is going to have to be a long, long way away. I once coached a trainer through a session in which the dog was in a dog run on a country road and would go berserk if someone walked down that road. The stranger could be as far as 250 feet away! Fortunately, it was possible to work on that road, and the treatment was successful. But some dogs only behave aggressively in the living room yet are insensitive to responses by the helper when he's halfway around the block. There have been times when I've had to talk to clients' neighbors and ask if we could walk up their driveways to do the work. Sometimes my first session with a family is all about setting up the training environment.

We will talk in greater detail on how to set up training scenarios in a later chapter, but right now let's walk through a few common situations in which family dogs behave aggressively and how CAT could be used in these situations. As I mentioned, the "type" of aggression your dog exhibits really refers to the situation in which he behaves aggressively. (Note: Do not start the work now. Just read this section and think about how you might arrange your setup.)

FURNITURE GUARDING

A dog named Magpie would often sit on the couch with one of her owners, Jennie, while she watched television. When Jennie's husband, Amos, would come over to sit down, Magpie would begin to bark fiercely and bare her teeth. While they used to laugh about it, it gradually became a greater concern when Magpie started snapping.

When the family decided to try CAT, they started by having Magpie wear her leash in the house for a few days. Amos approached the couch only close enough that Magpie knew he was there, and when she stopped staring at him or did anything a tiny bit more acceptable than

barking, he walked away. Remember, dogs usually don't offer great behavior right away, so you start out by having the helper walk away when the dog does something a teeny-tiny bit better, even if it's just stopping for two seconds instead of one between barks.

Amos repeated this several times. Once he could tell that Magpie was not worried about him at that distance, he came a short step closer. When he was ready to watch TV, either he sat in a chair rather than on the couch or Magpie and Jennie moved to the chair. If Magpie barked, stiffened, stared at Amos, or behaved in any way that was not friendly or neutral, Amos waited calmly; as soon as she stopped behaving aggressively and did something neutral or friendly, he walked away. It's important to understand that he always walked away when Magpie was behaving in desirable

ways. He did not walk away when she was behaving aggressively. In addition, he never walked closer to Magpie while she was on the couch if she had just behaved nicely because he knew that would be too much pressure for her, and he didn't want to mess up all the work he'd been doing.

After working with Magpie for a while like this, Jennie called Magpie off the couch, put her in her crate, and gave her a very delicious dog toy stuffed with a mix of wet and dry dog food so that she could entertain herself for a while as the couple watched TV. Each day, Amos did a few minutes of this work with Magpie until he could sit on the couch with her and his wife.

While they were doing the work, as Amos got close to the couch, at first he had to pretend that he was going to sit down rather than actually sitting down (kind of a fake-out) and then walk away when Magpie didn't behave aggressively. If he misinterpreted her comfort level, and she did behave aggressively, Jennie held onto the leash so that she couldn't move close enough to snap. When she did anything that was neutral or friendly, Amos walked away.

Every time Amos walked away, Jennie followed Magpie's lead. If she asked to be petted, she was petted. If she kept looking at Amos, Jennie just sat and waited. This process was inconvenient for Amos, who was often tired after work and just wanted to relax, but both Jennie and Amos knew that sometimes pet ownership requires some sacrifice, so they did the

work until things were comfortable in the family again.

During the same period of time that Amos was doing this work, Jennie worked on teaching Magpie to jump off the couch on cue when Jennie said "Off" (and gave her a treat when she responded correctly) and go into her crate on her own. To teach Magpie to jump off the couch, at first Jennie went to the kitchen and called Magpie to her. When Magpie jumped off the couch, Jennie gave her a very special treat instead of her daily kibble or her usual treats. Jennie chose the kitchen because she knew Magpie was always willing to go into the kitchen because of the possibility of treats or dropped food. The treats that Jennie offered for this training were extra-special (leftover meat from dinner, string cheese, liver treats) because she wanted to be sure that Magpie really liked cooperating. Jennie gave Magpie these special treats during intensive training but not at any other times.

Over time, Jennie could stand next to the couch and cue Magpie to get off the couch for a treat. Eventually, Jennie worked up to saying the cue, having Magpie jump off the couch and get a treat, and allowing her to jump right back up so that it never seemed like a punishment. Jennie repeated this exercise until Magpie knew the drill very well. Over time, Jennie would have Magpie stay on the floor longer and longer until she could wait on the floor while Jennie and Amos sat down on the couch to watch TV.

At this point, Magpie would only jump on the couch when invited by Jennie and Amos. If she was on the floor, either Amos or Jennie would say, "Up!" and give Magpie a treat as soon as she jumped onto the couch. Gradually, Magpie had to wait longer and longer for the cue to jump "up" so that she learned that it wasn't her decision when to jump up, it was her owners' decision. Normally, letting dogs get on the furniture is no problem if families enjoy it, but it was a big problem in Magpie's case because she guarded the seat. For this reason, she doesn't get to decide when she will join her family on the couch.

Eventually, Magpie learned to wait to be invited onto the couch. Jennie and Amos often cued her to get "off" the couch before Amos sat down, and then to get "up" on the couch only after he was seated and comfortable. Other times, they gave Magpie a food-stuffed dog toy in place of dinner, and she ate it in her crate while her people ate pizza on the couch; they did not want to add to the difficulties Magpie had in behaving properly on the couch.

All of these tools together provided the family with options and comfort while letting the dog understand that life can still be good even when it's not just Magpie and Jennie on the couch alone. You may have noticed that there were two parts to Maggie's training: Amos did the CAT procedure, and Jennie worked on teaching her to get off the couch and go into her crate for a treat. Together, these two techniques gave Magpie acceptable ways to behave during couch time.

GUESTS VISIT

When Victor's dog, Duke, heard the doorbell, he would go berserk, barking and circling. When Victor opened the door, Duke would often stare at the visitor while continuing to bark. The last time someone came to visit, Duke had charged the person; when the guest was turning to run away, Duke had bitten him on the back of the leg. Victor was very concerned about Duke's behavior and his friends' safety, so he asked some friends and family if they would be willing to help him work with Duke if he promised to have Duke safely secured and made them dinner. One of the hardest things to do is find helpers willing to work with aggressive or reactive dogs, so it's always nice to reward them, too!

When Victor found the first person who would do the work, and before they started to work, Victor set up the environment.

Before the helper was expected to arrive, Victor put Duke's leash on and took him for a walk to relieve himself. (It's hard for a dog to learn when has to go, so it's always good to take care of business first.) Then, Victor brought Duke back into the house and tethered him to a heavy clip he had installed in a stud in the wall. Duke could see the front door from his safe spot. Because Duke was a very strong dog, Victor decided this would be a safer approach than trying to hold the leash while also instructing his friends on what to do. In the days leading up to doing the work with Duke, Victor clipped Duke in this place for short periods of time at different times of day with a comfortable dog bed and a chew bone or treat-stuffed toy so that he got used to spending time there. If you have a piece of furniture heavy enough that your dog can't move it, you can opt for tethering him to that. The key is safety.

Victor double-checked that his dog's leash was secure enough to hold him. Earlier, when he had realized that if Duke wanted to get out of his collar badly enough, he could back out of it, Victor decided to get Duke used to a body harness. He used a clip to attach the leash to both the harness and the collar at the same time to reduce Duke's risk of getting loose. He had Duke wear this equipment at home and on walks for a while every day when they weren't doing any training so that Duke wouldn't associate it with the CAT treatment.

During the time before he was able start CAT with Duke, Victor put a note on his door saying, "Only ring once! Please be patient." This allowed Victor time to secure Duke in his safe spot with a treat before anyone came inside. Victor knew it was very important to ensure that Duke never bit anyone again, both for the guest's safety and for Duke's own safety.

As he prepared to do the procedure, Victor also spent time studying his dog's body language by doing the observation exercises so that he could work with his dog more effectively. He also studied general body-language information about dogs. (Something that smart animal trainers say is, "Know your species!") Most of us humans think we know dogs inside and out because we have been around them most of our lives. Unfortunately, we very often attribute human likes, dislikes, and behaviors to them. While many dogs fit in remarkably well with us, they are still dogs, and they need to be understood like dogs. If we "understand" them like something they're not, we are sure to run into problems.

Victor understood that each dog is an individual who may be aggressive his own way, and he also understood how aggression often presents itself in the canine species in general. He knew that, before he bites, a dog will often freeze, lower his head, look at the body part he is preparing to bite, and lunge forward. He may pull his tongue inside his mouth so he won't bite it and so his teeth are available to bite with.

Victor had videotaped Duke's behavior at the door a few times, so he knew that Duke usually turned in circles before freezing and lowering his head as someone came through the door. Victor knew that circling was part of his dog's chain of aggressive behaviors.

When Victor's friend Glenda approached the door to help with Duke's CAT training, Victor went to the door and greeted her as usual. They were great friends and often waved their arms and spoke in excited voices when they saw each other. When they did this, Victor observed that Duke became very agitated. He showed his agitation by drooling, circling, and barking repeatedly from his secured space. Victor realized this wasn't going to make it easy for Duke to make good choices at the door, so he decided it would be a good idea to make greetings a little less animated. This is similar in concept to starting out very far away. Too close can be too stressful for learning. Too active and loud can also be too stressful for learning. Start where the dog can be successful, and build from there.

By the end of the procedure, the goal was to have guests come in and greet Victor in their normal ways, but Victor knew that wasn't going to happen for a while. In this case, Glenda went back outside, and Victor greeted her outside with the door closed, with a quieter voice and less animation. He asked Glenda to text him when she arrived next time so he could meet her outside, where they could greet without upsetting Duke, and then they would calmly go into the house together.

Victor asked Glenda to walk away from the house, down the sidewalk leading to the front door, and stop near the street. He left the door open so Duke, from his safely tethered position, could see her. When she turned back to face the house from this farther distance, Duke could see her, but he didn't bark. They decided that this would be a great place to start the procedure. Victor knew how important it was to avoid the dog's becoming too worked up.

Victor made sure Duke was secured and then stood inside the door of the house. On Victor's instruction (they used cell phones), Glenda moved one step toward them. Duke's ears perked up, and he closed his mouth. Victor told Glenda to stay in place until Duke tried something different. Because Duke was not overly stressed, pretty soon he turned his head away, and Glenda immediately turned and walked away. Because it was hard for Glenda to see what Duke was doing in any detail, Victor instructed her by phone. This was fine for Duke because Victor often talked on the phone. Walking

away was a reward for Duke's turning his head rather than performing more of his series of aggressive behaviors. Before this day, Duke had always gotten the same reward of people turning to move away (quickly!) when he was aggressive, but now, instead, his gentler or neutral behaviors were being rewarded from a very easy distance.

Glenda made a mental note of how close she had come to the door the first time she approached. Many people use some sort of movable marker, like a piece of tape or a stone, to help them remember where they were so they don't accidentally go too close too soon, which can cause the dog to have an aggressive response. Glenda remembered exactly where she was by noticing a crack in the sidewalk. The next

time she approached Duke, she came one small step closer than before. Like the first time, she waited for Duke to offer an alternative to aggression. Victor told Glenda that the goal was for her to walk away when Duke was moving in some way rather than when he was being very still. If being still worked to get Glenda to walk away, Duke would continue being still, and it would become harder for Victor to find any behaviors to work with.

Things went very well for the next several approaches, with Glenda stepping a few inches closer each time. When Glenda got several steps closer, Duke suddenly erupted into an aggressive display that was pretty frightening. The first thing Glenda thought was that all this work had been for nothing. It can be very frustrating when you've been working along just fine and there is a sudden eruption of unpleasant behavior from the dog. What happened was simply that the situation had changed in some way. Possibly Glenda was now coming close enough that Duke was more worried and he behaved in his old way. It's also possible that the light outdoors had changed because the sun went behind a cloud, or any number of other things that changed the situation a little. This does not mean the procedure wasn't working. All it means is that something changed.

Victor understood, and he explained to Glenda that they would have to help Duke work through these new environmental conditions by doing the same procedure in the new conditions. It also was important to take it easy and try not to overwhelm Duke.

The next time Glenda approached, she didn't come as close as she had come when Duke behaved aggressively. She repeated her approach at this farther distance several times, watching for Duke to move his body loosely, turn away, sit, lie down, or do any safe, neutral, or friendly behaviors. Once he had done this several times, she and Victor agreed that she was going to come one step closer. She made the step very small. This time, it was a very successful attempt, so they all took a break. Duke got a bathroom break with Victor, followed by some water and playtime outside. After Duke was taken care of, Glenda and Victor sat outside with a nonalcoholic drink to talk over what they'd accomplished. (Drinking alcohol while training aggressive dogs is like drinking and driving. Don't do it!)

They started the work again after half an hour, repeating some of the steps they had just done and letting Duke have lots of successes. Then they called it a day and scheduled a new session for the following week.

Each week, they repeated the procedure. After several sessions, Glenda approached almost close enough for Duke to touch her, but not quite, so they decided it was time to take the show on the road. Victor took Duke's leash from its clip. Glenda walked out the front door. Victor and Duke followed Glenda from a very safe distance. Once outside, they walked up and down the sidewalk with several feet between

DOG PARKS

I'm going to take a detour into an area frequently associated with dog aggression just to get this out on the table. Earlier in the book, I told you about a pet owner whose dog began to behave aggressively toward other dogs soon after being attacked by two dogs in a dog park, and that the dog had become pushy and growly with other dogs on subsequent visits to the dog park. My response to this owner was, "Don't ever take your dog to the dog park." I wasn't saying that no dog should ever go to any dog park. I was saying that this dog should never go to any dog park. He had such a bad experience there that each visit was painful for him and further convinced him that other dogs were dangerous. There was no way to perform aggression work inside the dog park, where the behavior of the other dogs was hit or miss. It wasn't safe, and it was likely to make the dog's behavior worse.

Dog parks can be great fun, but they can also be dangerous and a place of high stress for dogs. You'll often see dogs in dog parks who are overly excited and too poorly behaved to be there. The fact is, many dogs don't really need to have dog friends. Some dogs really benefit from dog friends, but those dogs are usually not the ones that have aggression problems around other dogs.

Dogs need their owners to protect them from situations that are too overwhelming for them. The social life your dog has with you is the social life that is important to him. Taking him to dog parks isn't always in his best interest. My advice is to only enter dog parks when there are just a few dogs (no more than three or four) and the owners are actively watching their dogs. If any of the dogs in the dog park is wearing a shock collar or is being a bully, leash your dog and leave. If your dog is the bully, definitely leash your dog and leave! This happens. Once my own dog guarded a man he'd just met from the man's own six-month-old Golden Retriever puppy! It was terribly embarrassing, and I gave a quick apology and left. That wasn't behavior my dog needed to practice. It's nothing to be ashamed of, although it may be momentarily embarrassing. Just apologize if needed, and leave.

them and Glenda. Every once in a while, when Duke was behaving very well, Glenda turned and walked away from Duke and Victor. Then they continued their walk. Sometimes Glenda walked in front, sometimes she walked beside, and sometimes she walked behind.

As this work continued, Duke became increasingly curious about Glenda. He lengthened his neck and sniffed toward her and took a few steps closer. Glenda did not approach Duke yet. She let him sniff in her direction while Victor maintained control of the leash without pulling it too tight. (Many dogs have learned to behave aggressively when their leashes are pulled tight. Victor kept just enough tension in the leash that he could easily control Duke should Duke lunge.)

They did this several times before they determined that Duke was ready to sniff Glenda's hand, and Glenda was ready to

let him. Duke touched her hand with his nose, licked lightly, and backed up. Glenda walked away and they called it a day again so that the session could end on a positive note.

If Victor and Glenda had been able to do a whole-day session, the procedure may have gone more quickly, but because both of them had full-time jobs and other commitments, it just wasn't possible. They found that sometimes when they started a new session, they had to back up a little bit in their progress and not expect too much of Duke. Some weeks, he picked up right where they had left off, but other weeks, he seemed to have regressed. They knew they couldn't expect more of Duke than he was offering freely, so they were conservative in their starting points.

Over several weeks, Duke approached Glenda and allowed her to pet him. Sometimes he would even lie down beside her while Victor and Glenda talked. Victor had a lot of friends, so he managed to encourage several others to do the same thing Glenda had done. Each time, the procedure worked a little better and went a little faster as Duke began to understand that Victor's friends weren't threats.

Victor remained vigilant when people were around for the rest of Duke's life, even after his behavior improved. Often Duke was clipped near his dog bed with a chew toy so that Victor could entertain guests or watch TV with a friend and not be 100-percent focused on Duke. Other times, he crated Duke in a separate room where Duke could relax. Victor never treated this as a punishment for Duke but instead as an opportunity to make having guests over less stressful.

Over time, Duke became much more comfortable about visitors. Victor invited his guests to drop treats near Duke but not overtly engage with him. Victor remained Duke's advocate and asked that people not lean over him, hug him, or otherwise do anything that might cause Duke to become overwhelmed and perhaps return to his history of biting.

AGGRESSION TOWARD OTHER DOGS

One common situation in which dogs behave aggressively is when they see strange dogs. Many dogs don't have much experience with other dogs, so their stress increases in their presence. Sometimes dogs like certain dogs but not others. And sometimes dogs don't like other dogs for some reason we may never fully understand. If the goal of the dog's aggressive behavior is to chase the other dog away, we can do the CAT procedure to help him learn how to behave safely in the presence of other dogs.

Lillie's dog, Beau, would bark viciously when he saw other dogs on leash on their walks. Lillie recruited a friend with a very friendly dog to help her work with Beau. Before their first work session, Lillie ensured that Beau's leash was secured on his harness and collar and that she felt comfortable holding him back if he should lunge.

Lillie had her friend, John, bring his dog, Belle, to the far corner of the street before she walked out her door with Beau. When Beau reacted aggressively to the sight of Belle, Lillie just casually stood still and waited until Beau produced a neutral or alternative behavior, and she used her cell phone to call John and have him stay where he was while she and Beau walked farther away from them. Several times, she slowed down and asked Beau to turn around with her, and they would walk a few steps toward John and Belle. She never dragged or forced Beau; she simply invited him to go the other way for a few steps. When Beau was far enough away from Belle that he displayed no aggression, Lillie let John know to start walking the opposite way at a moderate pace. Now they were all walking in the same direction, with John and Belle in front. They stayed a block ahead of

Beau and Lillie for a while and gradually reduced the distance. Lillie wanted Beau to be able to see Belle as they walked so he wouldn't find her as threatening.

As the work proceeded, Lillie sped up just slightly and John slowed down just slightly so that the dogs were a little closer to each other. If it got to the point that Beau froze, growled, or otherwise expressed concerns about Belle up there ahead of him, Lillie walked slowly along until he chose a safer behavior.

As long as Beau didn't try to charge the duo ahead of them, Lillie allowed him to make any of a variety of choices as long as they were safe or neutral. If he turned away, great! Lillie turned away, too, and they walked in the other direction. If he stared, Lillie waited for him to break his stare and either followed Beau away from Belle or just didn't make Beau walk forward while John and Belle continued to move, increasing the distance between them in that way. Lillie never forced Beau to do anything unless she had to break up a dangerous situation. She let Beau learn that he could make effective choices that weren't aggressive and that his safe choices would not result in punishment, correction, or pain.

As you can see, this scenario is a little different than the first two, and there are some reasons behind that. For one thing, we still want Beau to know that making good choices is going to pay off in the reward of putting more distance between him and the other dog. While Amos was able to reward Magpie's better behaviors by walking away from the couch, Magpie had little space to move, so Amos showed her that she could control the environment in ways that were worthwhile to her by choosing nicer behavior. But Amos was the one to go away. When we're out walking our dogs on the street, we can't control what other people will do with their dogs. We can't expect strangers to automatically walk away when our dog is good. They're far more likely to expect us to punish our dog for his aggressive behavior, even though we know that punishment can easily worsen the behavior.

If Beau decides that he can't make that other dog go away, so he'll just go away himself, who are we to argue? Let him! Go with him! Your walk doesn't have to be linear and always go in the same direction. It should show your dog that aggression is not the only way to get relief from other dogs who make him uncomfortable. Turning the other cheek works, too. If working with a helper and his or her dog, you can reset the situation to show your dog that it works again and again, in this location and that, when it's dusk and when it's midday. The advantage of doing some work with a friend and his or her nice dog is that you can set up some situations that you know you'll need to train, and you can repeat them until your dog gets the idea that it's all good. That's very helpful.

You can also set up some more formal training scenarios with your friend and his or her dog, and later with other dogs, that will help the process move along faster. Lillie and Beau will stand in one place while John and Belle approach from a great distance. They will do what Glenda did in the setup with Victor and Duke. They'll come just a little closer, and then, when Beau is being a very good boy, they will reward him by walking away again. Lillie will let Beau watch them walk away because seeing them walk away is a huge reward. She won't call, talk to, or distract Beau at that point. If he turns to her, she will talk calmly to him or pet him briefly. Remember, she's rewarding his safe, friendly, or neutral behavior; she's not forcing him to do what she wants him to do. John and Belle will gradually inch closer and walk away again and again. If Beau reacts aggressively on one of the approaches, John and Belle wait until he does something safe or neutral before walking away. Belle always gets petting, treats, and reassurance from John throughout the procedure, especially if Beau is growly. But if Beau checks in with Lillie, he also gets petted and reassured. He does not get treats just yet because we want to teach him how to make other dogs go away by being nice. If he likes treats, he can get plenty of treats and petting for doing easy tricks and for lying calmly in his bed or next to Lillie on the couch after the training session. Treats are a great training tool, but right now we want him to see what else the environment can give him.

These are just a few examples of how you might set up a training session for your own dog by recruiting friends and getting creative about how to use the environment in which the aggression usually occurs. If at any point you are confused, take a break and think it through some more. Don't take risks that could push your dog further than he can tolerate.

9

SAFETY
AND
MANAGEMENT

During the writing of this book, I was bitten by a dog while performing the CAT procedure. It was the second time in twelve years of doing this work. After the first bite, years ago, which happened while I was talking to one owner and not paying enough attention to what the other owner was doing with the dog on the leash, I became very cautious and ensured that I set up a very safe training environment before I started to work. The first bite resulted in some bruising but no broken skin because I had been wearing a thick sweatshirt. I did mourn the loss of a favorite sweatshirt, but I only got a bruise. It was a good trade-off.

The more recent bite was on the bare skin of my forearm and resulted in an ER visit, antibiotics, significant bruising, some deep scrapes from his teeth, one deep puncture wound, and scarring. I got X-rays to ensure that no broken tooth fragments had been left in my flesh and that the tooth had not nicked my bone. A nurse thoroughly cleaned my wounds. I got no stitches because the doctor preferred to leave bite wounds open unless they were gaping so that the germs from the dog's mouth could drain. There was quite a bit of bleeding the day it happened, and then it oozed for a few days more. The doctor prescribed Tramadol for the pain. I'm just glad it wasn't my face.

It is utterly essential to understand that when you are working with dogs with aggression, there is always a risk involved. If your dog has never bitten anyone, there's always a first time. I've been bitten only twice, although there were plenty of close calls. I know other trainers who have been bitten many more times.

Most trainers who work with aggressive animals are bitten once in a while. Although working with aggressive dogs means that bites might happen, I must stress that if you hear of a trainer who is being bitten all the time, or one who uses his or her bite scars as badges of honor, you may need to consider a different trainer. Whether you are a dog-behavior professional or a pet owner, the highest badge of honor is no one being bitten by a dog, ever. If you or someone else is bitten, this is an opportunity to learn and plan. A trainer or pet owner who is bitten often is not taking appropriate precautions to minimize the risk of a bite and is putting people and the dog at risk. This person may push a dog harder than he can deal with while learning new ways to behave.

In working with a dog who displays aggression, there is a risk that someone may be bitten, of course. That person may lose some blood, experience some pain, and carry around some anxiety about the incident. In some cases, a person working with an aggressive dog may be killed, with children and elderly people at the greatest risk. It's usually a familiar dog that who bites someone; family members or other people who know the dog are most likely to be bitten—although dogs bite strangers, too.

It sounds awful for me to be saying all this stuff about how much harm a dog can do when I'm writing about a treatment for canine aggression. But the fact is that there is real and significant risk, and I'm not going to skip over it just because talking about it is uncomfortable. It's realistic. It is not just big dogs or those breeds that are vilified in our communities, such as Pit Bulls and Rottweilers, who bite. In fact, Pit Bulls are often blamed for incidents involving mixed-breed dogs or dogs whose breeds are unknown. In popular media, if it's the size of a Pit Bull or the color of a Pit Bull (meaning any color), has short hair, and maybe has a blocky head, they call it a Pit Bull. But I'm sorry to tell you that little Dachshunds and Pomeranians have killed children, too. The beloved Golden Retriever and his cousin, the Labrador, have killed people. At the same time, some of the nicest dogs I've ever known were Pit Bulls. Just because a dog has the capacity to cause harm doesn't mean that he will.

THE DOG'S HISTORY

Something you have to consider when deciding whether to train your own aggressive dog is his history. What did you answer in the previous chapter? Has your dog ever bitten before? How hard? Has he ever been taught to bite on purpose?

The second dog who bit me was a German Shepherd Dog who had been shipped to the United States from Germany as a young puppy. He had been trained briefly for Schutzhund, a sport intended to "evaluate the temperament, character, trainability, and mental and physical soundness" of the German Shepherd Dog, according to the United Schutzhund Clubs of America. (Other

Schutzhund is protection-dog training that includes bite work. The trainers wear bite sleeves and other safety gear.

breeds participate in Schutzhund, but it was developed for German Shepherd Dogs). The protection component of the training is considered necessary to teach the dog the discernment needed to identify those who are threats and those who are not. While many dogs can be trained to a level of control that ensures they never harm anyone, I strongly disagree that any dog, protection breed or otherwise, should be left to his own devices to determine who is risky and decide how to act on it. You are the one that has to be responsible.

After the German Shepherd bit me, I spent a great deal of time thinking about what I did wrong. I always take it on my shoulders when a session isn't successful. What did I miss? What could I have done differently? What can I do differently next time? When a person is bitten in a training situation, it is usually because the person didn't understand something

PROTECTED CONTACT

I strongly advise you to use extreme caution if you are working with a dog who has had any kind of protection training. Do not work alone; partner with a trainer experienced in using modern positive methods to deal with aggression. Do not work without a muzzle on the dog. When working a dog with a protection-dog history, employ *protected contact*. Protected contact is a zoo practice in which animals with the potential to behave dangerously are on one side of a secure barrier appropriate to the species, and the trainer and everyone else are on the other side. The barrier must be robust, secure, and tall enough that the dog cannot escape from it.

If you are working with a smaller dog, there are a wide variety of ways to incorporate protected contact to prevent him from harming someone during training. Leashes, exercise pens, and baby gates may do the trick. If you are working with a massive, powerful dog, your options are more limited. A 2-pound Chihuahua can be on a harness with his leash slipped under a chair leg. A 200-pound English Mastiff with aggression may require some serious fence work. If the dog is a champion escape artist, a 4-foot chain link fence isn't going to work. In many cases, the dog will be on leash, but the leash must be held by someone who is strong enough to control the dog and will stay tuned in to the work. Otherwise, you must secure the dog to a stationary object that the dog cannot pull over with the full power of his lunging strength.

that was happening, let his or her guard down, or intentionally provoked the bite. I assure you that I did not intentionally provoke a bite, and I was tuned in to the training.

Let me be perfectly clear that I believe I was fully informed of this German Shepherd Dog's history, and I believe the trainer and pet owner I worked with to be responsible and reliable. However, the dog's behavior was neither reliable nor consistent. I had worked with him on one previous occasion, and the work that day had gone beautifully. Before we finished a short session on that occasion, he approached me, licked my hand, and nuzzled it. The second time I saw him, after an hour of work, he seemed to be approaching to greet me. His body language was loose, and then he suddenly launched himself and bit my arm as if I were wearing a bite suit. Neither the owner nor I saw it coming. The trainer was holding the dog's leash and instantly began pulling him away, so her view of what happened was not as clear. Without the leash and the trainer's quick actions, the bite would have been much more serious. Following the incident, while I was being bandaged, I said several times, "I misread his body language. I missed something." The

Small dogs can have big bites, but they are generally easier to manage because of their small size. However, this doesn't mean that we can safely ignore their behavior.

owner said, "I didn't see that coming. He seemed fine." It was a case of "he was fine until he wasn't."

After much consideration, I believe that I inadvertently cued the dog to bite me by lifting my arm so that my forearm was parallel to the floor. I am not a Schutzhund trainer, and I don't know the training practices of the sport, but after interviewing several trainers, it is my understanding that a Schutzhund dog should bite only the bite sleeve and only on command. I have heard and read about a few dogs who aren't interested in the sleeve and go for the person instead. It is possible that I inadvertently invited the dog to bite me, not knowing that the motion of my arm could cue a bite, and that the dog had not been trained to withhold his bite without the bite sleeve. Dogs don't always respond to the intended commands; they may make other connections and respond to other things

in the environment, even accidental or coincidental things.

This German Shepherd Dog's behavior had to do with his own unique personal history of training. He had bitten other people before me, and, from what I learned about his previous bite incidents, I believe that some of them were distancing bites. In other words, his goal was to subdue a person or to chase someone away. This is probably why the CAT procedure worked well the first time I saw him. But the dog had learned some different things that are hard to untangle. This dog had been removed from Schutzhund training before I met him because he didn't have the desired qualities. Again, I urge you to avoid doing CAT with a dog who has been trained for any kind of bite work because the dog's commands or cues may not be clear enough to determine what he is trying to achieve with his behavior.

SETTING UP FOR SAFETY

As you're getting your head around whether or not you will be doing CAT work with your dog, let's talk further about how you're going to set the stage for safety for you, your dog, the people or animals your dog wants relief from, and bystanders.

The very first thing to do is to muzzle-train your dog, even if he has not yet bitten anyone. I previously mentioned trainer Chirag Patel's video, "Teaching a Dog to Wear a Muzzle," available on YouTube. Look it up and watch it (about fifteen times!). It's an excellent tutorial on how to teach your dog to wear a muzzle comfortably. I recommend that you get a basket muzzle similar to the one in this video. If you can't find one locally, they are available online. The basket-style muzzle will allow your dog to breathe freely, drink, and even eat treats while wearing it, but it will prevent your dog from doing serious harm to anyone he may feel overwhelmed enough to bite. Some bruising may occur if a dog punches you with a muzzle, but it's much better than if he gets a hold of your skin with his teeth.

If you cannot muzzle your dog, call a positive-reinforcement trainer to help. Search for trainers at the following websites: the Association of Professional Dog Trainers (www.apdt.com), the International Association of Animal Behavior Consultations (www.iaabc. org), the Pet Professional Guild (www. petprofessionalguild.com), or the Karen Pryor Academy (www.karenpryoracademy. com). You will likely do the hands-on work of muzzle training under this trainer's guidance. If the trainer is not familiar with Chirag Patel's video, show it to him or her so that the trainer knows that this is the kind of training you are looking for.

Dogs should be taught to wear muzzles during easy times when nothing upsetting is going on. If you introduce the muzzle right before an aggression-training session or at a time when the dog is likely to behave aggressively based on his past history, he will learn to associate the muzzle with those occasions. What you want is a dog who can comfortably wear a muzzle when he goes for a walk, goes to the vet,

Fences for any dogs must be sturdy, secure, and escape-proof.

when guests are in your home, or when you'll be entering an unknown situation.

When I adopted my lovely Greyhound, Bravo, she was sent home with a basket muzzle just because all retired racing Greyhounds are sent home with a basket muzzle. Because Greyhounds often have strong prey drives (chasing and killing is rewarding for many of them), I was advised to keep her in the muzzle for at least two weeks until we saw how she would behave around my cats. She never for an instant behaved aggressively toward them (and, in fact, was initially a little afraid of them), but it was a very good bit of safety advice that my family took to heart. My Greyhound wore her muzzle occasionally throughout her life, depending on what was going on. It was something she was familiar with from her racing days, and she never objected or

seemed to mind wearing it. If you train your dog the right way, he will always associate muzzles with good experiences. Once your dog is muzzle-trained, have him wear the muzzle at random times in addition to times when he might need it for safety so that it always seems natural and even random.

You can do outdoor CAT with a fence between the dog and the helper dog or person. The fence needs to be sturdy and secure so that the dog cannot escape by digging under, jumping over, or breaking through. If a gate is involved, secure it *with a lock* before commencing the training.

For a small dog, work with him on leash. The leash should be of an appropriate size for the dog. If the dog tends to chew on the leash and there is any risk of him biting through, putting two leashes on the dog can give you backup. You may also cover the foot or so of leash near the dog's collar with a section of PVC or rubber pipe, such as an old garden hose.

The owner and the helpers are advised to wear long pants and flat, closed-toe shoes during the first part of this work. This is a tricky area if you have a dog who only behaves aggressively toward people in high heels and skirts, but chances are it will work fine. Eventually, your helper will need to wear the kind of clothing that people are wearing when the aggression occurs, if it makes a difference to the dog. The way you tell if whether it makes a difference to the dog is simply by observing and asking yourself, "Does the aggression happen toward people when they're wearing this kind of clothing but not that kind?" If the dog is aggressive no matter what they're wearing, this isn't an issue. Either way, for starters, I would like you to protect your legs from

bites. Arm covering is helpful as well, even if you're working in temperatures too hot to wear a jacket or sweatshirt; the extra clothing may protect your arms. At the animal shelters where I work, we like to use fingerless protective wildlife sleeves that go up to the elbow or slightly above. The fingers are free so that we can perform all the tasks that need to be done, but the forearm, which is the most commonly bitten part of the body, is covered.

Think about any other situations you may need to manage based on your observations of your dog's behavior and get creative to make safety and management tactics part of your training. Over time, as you are successful doing things one way, you'll need to switch up the environment several times to help the dog learn that his new behavior works in whatever conditions are present.

10

TRAINING TEAM, TOOLS, AND LOCATION

I f you've decided that you're willing and able to do CAT work safely with your dog, start planning and preparing. You will need reliable people who can participate in the work with you. If your dog behaves aggressively toward other dogs, you will need a confident, calm dog to work with a competent, reliable handler. A trainer has actually used a cat as the helper because the dog behaved aggressively toward cats, but this was a confident cat who was accustomed to wearing a harness and leash, and while the dog was noisy toward the cat, the trainer did not anticipate that he would harm the cat. This type of work was performed by a skilled trainer, and it is definitely not recommended for you if you're new to CAT training.

When preparing for CAT, you'll need a variety of tools, and you'll need to know where you are going to perform the work.

HELPERS

In canine aggression work, the people and animals who act in place of the person or animal toward whom your dog behaves aggressively are called by a variety of names. It doesn't really matter what you call your team (usually a human and a dog), but if you're talking with other trainers, you may hear them use different terms. I've heard them called *decoy dogs*, and I used to use this term myself. I tried calling them *actors*, because their job basically is to play a role, but people seemed to feel too much pressure, as if we were going to do give out Oscars later or something. The last thing we want to do is add unnecessary pressure to our team. So, I've settled on the term *helpers*, a term that dog trainers and behaviorists understand and that is clear to the people who will help perform the work of training your dog to behave more safely.

Human helpers must be willing to work under your supervision. Ideally, they should be willing to read and discuss this book with you. Both you and your helpers need to study canine body language and behavior and to perform the observation exercises described earlier in the book. You need to trust that your helpers will follow your instructions and not change the game plan unless there is an unexpected safety risk. If they don't follow your instructions, you may end up with a mess that won't help your dog or you and may even make things worse. Human helpers should not be afraid of dogs but should have a healthy respect for the damage a dog of any size can do. A lot of people are convinced they have a special connection with dogs and that all dogs like them. This is 100 percent false no matter who says it (and a lot of people do!).

The first sheltering organization where I worked originally had two shelters. The dogs there usually start to like the behavior specialists before they like anyone else in our organization. However, these behavior specialists do not assume that the dogs would never bite them if they were overwhelmed. The behavior specialists have learned to adjust their own behavior to minimize stress to the animals. They hand out tons of treats when it's appropriate. The animals learn to trust them, and this can seem almost magical sometimes. But it's not magic, or calm assertive energy, or anything mystical. It's skill.

If your dog behaves aggressively toward all unfamiliar humans, you just need to find any human who is trustworthy and follows instructions well. The person should also have the ability to work for a while without getting overly tired.

A lot of dogs pick very specific kinds of humans or animals they don't like. A lot of times, it's men (sorry, guys), but it can also be women or children. This may sound strange, but a dog can dislike people wearing hats; people of a certain race; people with disabilities, who may move, sound, or act differently from most of the

If men in hats are your dog's trigger, your helper should be a man wearing a hat.

people with whom the dog is familiar and comfortable; and even his own beloved owner if the owner is on a skateboard or wearing a costume, for example.

Mary, a dog I worked with in a seminar setting, was aggressive toward people who had recently used weed trimmers. She didn't like the person while he or she was using it, and she continued to hold a grudge after he or she put the weed trimmer away. Our CAT work was very successful.

Some dogs behave aggressively toward very specific people in very specific situations. Other dogs respond to changes. Sometimes you'll find that bundling up for the winter causes your dog to behave differently around you. It's even common for a dog to have a problem with one family member and no one else. We once got a call from a man whose large dog guarded the dog food and dog bed from him, but his wife could do anything she wanted with the dog.

For a dog-aggressive dog, try working with a fake dog—the more lifelike, the better.

As we discussed earlier, doing the work with children is risky. Neither I nor the publisher of this book condones working with children without the help of a professional who has the kids' interest foremost in his or her mind.

Good helper dogs are difficult to find because people with nice dogs don't want to expose them to risky situations. Often, trainers are the ones who will use their own dogs as helpers because they know what they are doing and have safety skills in their tool kit.

The first helper dog to introduce to your dog is a fake dog. Melissa & Doug™ is a toy company that makes nearly life-sized, realistic-looking fake dogs. Although they are sold as toys, I consider them working equipment. I recommend putting the fake dog away when you're not using it so that it remains a useful tool for working with your dog. Melissa & Doug makes a variety of stuffed dog breeds, ranging from Jack Russell Terriers to Rottweillers. The fake dog I've had the most success with is the Husky. More dogs have behaved the way they behave around real dogs toward the Husky. Often, these tools can result in some really important and interesting responses that will help set up the training environment.

The biggest advantage of using fake dogs is that no other dogs can get hurt, and you can do more observations to see what your dog is likely to do in the presence of another dog. You've likely already seen his behavior with other dogs, but in the moment, when you're preoccupied with ending the interaction and keeping everyone safe, it's hard to really look at it closely. I used to be skeptical about using fake dogs, but I've since changed my mind. We use these dogs very often in our shelter work, and some dogs will attack a fake dog and not give up, just as if it were a fighting dog or a prey animal. I don't recommend using fake dogs in all of the work you're going to do with your dog, but it's a good way to get started and see how your dog is going to respond under different conditions. This is also a great way to practice setting up your training space and how to move during the work before introducing real dogs to the situation.

Helper dogs are treasures, and you should treat them well. The ideal helper dog will not respond aggressively when another dog is behaving aggressively in his presence or even toward him. This dog will be calm and responsive to his owner. He won't be overly fearful. He will ideally respond well to treats or petting from his owner so he can be rewarded frequently for the hard job he's doing—and this is not a job that a dog can or should do for a long time over and over.

It is possible to ruin a helper dog by convincing him that the world is full of dangerous dogs and that he'd better chase them away. The helper dog could end up needing CAT training himself! This has not happened to a helper dog I've worked with, but it can definitely happen if you do not tend to the helper

Watch for signs of fear in your helper dog.

dog's behavioral responses. For example, if your helper dog is showing signs of fear (cowering, shaking, trying to hide or escape), he needs a break or he needs to retire from this work. Any helper dog should be retired after several sessions with aggressive dogs, no matter how successful his work has been. Remember the character Data from Star Trek? He was a lifelike human-made being called an *android*, and I've often commented that we need an android dog that can respond just as a given dog needs it to respond, but with no emotional repercussions. If any of you are working on such a product, I am interested!

Sometimes a helper dog seems great at the beginning of a session but begins to respond aggressively to the other dog's aggression as you progress. You must retire this helper dog immediately for his own well-being and to avoid the risk of a real dogfight during training.

Keeping training sessions short, no longer than forty-five minutes or an hour at the most, when using a helper dog is a good practice to consider. Some helper dogs need even shorter sessions. Some can do multiple very short (fifteen-minute) sessions throughout a day, but you may need longer sessions to make progress with the aggressive dog.

Reward your helper dog often during the training and afterward and make sure there is water available. Often when my Greyhound, Bravo, was my helper, I would take her to a park for a relaxing walk after a training session, or I would let her play with other friendly dogs.

TRAINING GEAR FOR CAT

Your aggressive dog must wear appropriate gear and equipment so that you can control him and prevent him from causing injury to himself or anyone in the training environment. Even if your dog has never bitten anyone, you need to be able to ensure that he never does.

The essential piece of equipment is a well-fitted collar with a sturdy (preferably metal) buckle. Leather or nylon collars are the best. A well-fitted collar will buckle snugly enough that it can't be pulled off over the top of the dog's head. Some dogs try to back out of their collars when on leash, and this poses a clear risk both for the dogs and anyone the dogs may behave aggressively toward. Some dogs will run off and be difficult to catch. Others will use the opportunity to attack. Neither is acceptable.

If you can't find a collar with a metal buckle, a sturdy plastic buckle will be OK, but test it for two things before you put it on your dog: (1) Clasp the buckle

securely without putting it on the dog and try to pull it open with your hands by yanking hard in opposite directions. Don't use the collar if it comes apart as you do this. (2) Check to see if the size on an adjustable collar increases with pressure. Some collars, especially cotton or fabric ones, will not hold their size and should only be used as a place to hang tags, not as handling gear. If you start out with this kind of collar well-fitted, but your dog pulls against it, it may end up large enough for him to get out of. Don't use the collar if it won't hold its size.

If you have a skinny-headed dog like a Greyhound, Afghan, or Rough Collie, or a dog with a very thick ruff of fur or a muscular neck, you may find that even if the collar is fitted just right, the dog can still pull out of it. Rough Collies have both a skinny head and a thick ruff, so their gear needs to be especially carefully considered. For dogs with necks the same size or bigger than their heads, there is a collar option called a *martingale* or *limited-slip* collar. Do not get the chain kind; get the nylon kind. This type of collar is designed to tighten up as the dog pulls, but you will size it so that it can't pull tightly enough to choke the dog. Read the fitting instructions carefully. A martingale collar once saved my Greyhound when we were taking a walk

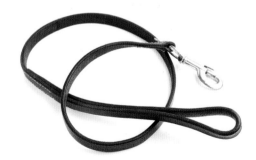

and an old car backfired right next to her. She jumped to bolt straight into traffic, but the collar was correctly fitted so she could not slip out of it. Although I had a

DON'T TOUCH

A sign on your dog's gear can be a good idea if your dog will have to go outside where you can't protect him from other dogs. The Yellow Dog Project suggests using a yellow ribbon or bandana to indicate that the dog "needs space," but not everyone knows about this. It's ideal to let your dog exercise and relieve himself in a private area, such as a fenced backyard, but that's not always possible. People who live in apartments have to walk their dogs several times a day. A warning for apartment dwellers might make walking their dogs a little easier. Consider a flag on your dog's leash or vest that says, "In Training: Do Not Touch." Of course, do not label your dog as a dangerous dog, which could make you a target of harrassment. Also, never try to pass any dog off as a service dog; this makes life a lot more difficult for people who have trained service dogs and need their dogs to have access to public spaces.

whirling dervish on my leash for a few seconds, she was safe, so I am a fan of this style of collar for some dogs.

However, I have an even stronger preference for body harnesses on most dogs. The incident with my Greyhound that I just mentioned is the reason I switched to a harness. There are several styles, so use the style that fits your dog's body best. For lean, deep-chested dogs like Greyhounds or Great Danes, I have found that a basic H-shaped harness works well. For a dog who pulls, there are a number of no-pull styles. The ideal is to use a harness that your dog will wear routinely, not just during CAT training. We don't want him to get the idea that the harness means the scary thing is going to happen, and we can prevent this by having him wear the harness at different times. I prefer a harness because no matter how careful you are, once in a while either you're going to accidentally let the dog get overwhelmed or something you could never have predicted is going to happen. A harness is hard for many dogs to escape from. Some dogs can, but you can purchase a little clip that will connect the leash to both the harness and the collar for double protection.

I am not a great fan of head harnesses for aggression work except occasionally with dogs who are already experienced in wearing them. I have seen dogs with aggression lunge into those things and throw their body weight into their upper necks, which are cranked around. Not only could a dog hurt himself this way

Head halters present some challenges, especially with aggressive dogs.

(and I know of some that have), but the sudden whipping around that happens when he lunges can make the entire situation even more aversive. That's not our goal. Our goal is to show the dog that he doesn't need to be worried. However, if your dog is already comfortable wearing a head halter and will be wearing it outside of training and after you've finished the CAT training, you can use the head halter but connect your leash to a collar rather than the halter. Do not use a style of halter that has to be very snug against the jaw joint to fit properly, as that can increase stress. Another challenge with the head halter is that some dogs can pull out of them. The solution here is to make sure it's fitted well and use a clip with a nylon strap to connect it to the collar or body harness. These can be found in some pet-supply stores and online.

Prong collars, shock collars, and slip leads *are absolutely not acceptable for* *this work*. They cause pain or discomfort, and we don't want to strengthen the connection between the scary person or dog and a negative sensation from the collar. People may tell you that these items do not cause discomfort if used

DID YOU KNOW?

If you work in shorter sessions, it is often necessary to backtrack a bit in your next session to work back up to the point you reached in your previous session. It's not the end of the world, but understanding that this could happen will make it less stressful for you. The dog will simply be getting extra chances to practice, and that's a good thing.

Make modifications as needed if your dog is a strong puller.

properly, but they absolutely do. This is why they are used in punishment-based training methods. If you're already using one of these collars, discontinue its use now. Instead of a prong collar, use a harness clipped to a collar. If your dog is an inveterate puller, do some work on leash handling before you begin CAT, even if you start out by just walking around your own backyard.

DID YOU KNOW?

A dog can figure out that if he tries to go to sleep, you might cut the session short. I've known some dogs who learned to instantly lie down and act sleepy as soon as they realized we were going to do CAT sessions—even before we did any work.

As discussed in the chapter on safety, a muzzle is an important piece of equipment. The dog should be trained to wear it in advance of aggression training so that he does not think it's any big deal to have it on. Some people are concerned that seeing their dog in a muzzle will make other people think he is aggressive. Chances are, if you're reading this book, you already have your own concerns in this area. If anyone asks you about it, and the situation is calm enough, just say, "He wears it to remind people not to touch him while he's training." Try not to be rude with people, but be prepared to be assertive. It's amazing how much everyone else in the world knows about your dog, right? If anyone tries to approach your dog or touch him, be his advocate and say, "Stop. Don't touch my dog."

If your dog is super-strong, or if you or another person who will be handling your dog has a strong history of yanking on the leash to correct the dog's behavior, you may need to attach his leash to a sturdy post, piece of furniture, or fence for training, depending on the situation you will be working in. Pulling on the leash is a very common habit that takes dog owners some practice to change. Securing the dog to something sturdy during training will give the owner or handler some time to practice not yanking the collar while ensuring security and safety for all involved with the CAT work. If the dog needs to move to a new training scenario, consider connecting his leash to your belt, so that the dog is connected to your center of gravity and cannot escape, yet you are still free to move with the dog. This is another way to work on teaching not to pull hard on the leash, too.

Bring some comfortable, portable chairs if you are going to have long sessions or if any of the participants have physical limitations. It is perfectly fine to work for a few hours as long as all dogs and people have access to water and can take regular breaks. Breaks are helpful for the dog, and they give the people a chance to review what has happened so far and make changes if needed. Although it is fine and often necessary to conduct shorter sessions, sometimes you can accomplish more in longer sessions. Sometimes a dog will begin to act tired partway through a session, and he probably is, but if the handler walks him around a bit, the dog can continue to learn. While we want to minimize the dog's stress, we can't completely eliminate it, or he can't learn.

REWARDABLE BEHAVIOR

It's very important to collect those friendly and neutral responses when you're starting out, but, over time, as you work the CAT procedure, your rewardable criteria are going to change. Undesirable behavior is pretty easy to figure out, but sometimes a behavior seems benign and not worth reinforcing when in fact it could be very useful in the process. I would much rather have a dog lick his lips rather than growl, so if he's been growling for the last two approaches but licks his lips on the third, take it! Walk away. You will hear people say that lip-licking is a "calming signal" and that it indicates stress. I don't necessarily disagree. I just know it's preferred by owners over growling, so I'm going to reinforce it. Later, you will stop walking away when he licks his lips and look for something different, like sitting or walking away.

This is true of every single aggression training method that exists.

OTHER TRAINING ESSENTIALS

PLACE MARKERS

As the helper approaches the dog each time, the person needs to know how close he or she came the previous time. If the helper was 20 feet away on one approach but forgot where he or she was the next time (it happens!) and approached to 17 feet away, this could be far too much for the dog and is likely to provoke an aggressive response.

If there are clear markers on the ground, such as tiles, the helper must pay close attention to which tile he or she walked up to. If the helper will be walking along a sidewalk or working on carpeting, or if your dog is just extremely sensitive to changes, as many herding dogs are, the helper may need to carefully mark each approach. I've used everything from sticky notes to pennies to pebbles. I even made a set of small beanbags, but the dogs I used them with seemed to get very distracted by them. Once, I laid a long measuring tape along the edge of the sidewalk and secured it with stones. This was very precise, but if someone had accidentally touched and retracted it, the sudden noise and movement could have caused a setback. Select your marking devices carefully, and

make sure you have a way to mark how close the helper is getting to the dog.

DATA COLLECTION SHEETS

Make sheets on which you can list the friendly and neutral behaviors you are looking for in one column and aggressive behaviors in the other. The goal, as you know, is to see more friendly and neutral behaviors and fewer aggressive ones. You can make your list using the observations you made in your earlier observation exercises.

PROTECTIVE GEAR

Fencing and other barriers are sometimes necessary when there's a chance a dog may bite or when aggression normally occurs at the fence. Sometimes, the dog will need to be set up on one side of a fence with his owner. If a dog whips around and nips or bites the handler in excitement, while it's not an ideal situation, he will need to be alone on one side of the fence. The owner or handler can be nearby but on the other side of the fence for safety, or the dog can be tethered in the area with the owner or handler nearby but not close enough to be bitten. We need the owner or handler to be nearby if he or she is normally nearby when the dog behaves aggressively.

If the dog is small or his bites are normally not hard, the handler may wear pants or boots and long sleeves or even wildlife-protection gloves. Gloves with bite flaps are especially helpful; each glove has a rectangle of leather extending from above the knuckles so that in case the dog decides

TRY AGAIN

If you get to a point in a training session where you're not making progress and can't figure out why, take a break or end the work for the day and try to figure out how to tweak your approach before your next training session.

to bite, he's going to get a mouth full of that flap rather than a mouth full of you. Seriously, as someone who had a rather impressive bite, you don't want to join the club. And if you're already in it, the goal is to graduate from it! Don't be afraid or embarrassed to wear protective gear. At the same time, don't let your protective gear make you overconfident, and don't assume that it won't hurt the dog to be pushed harder because he can't hurt you. The goal is to help the dog learn that there are things he can do other than aggression, not to push him to the point of reacting.

11

THE CAT PROCEDURE

The constructional approach defines most good reinforcement-based training techniques. You first clearly identify what is happening now. Then you clearly define where you'd like to end up when the training is done. In other words, you decide what you want the dog to do instead of aggression. As you go along, you determine how you'll get from here to there and how to maintain the change. In a sense, this means that the training never ends.

As you prepare to work on your dog's aggression, ask yourself these questions:

1. What behavior is happening now?
   a. What problem behavior is happening?
   b. How bad is this behavior?
   c. Who is around when it happens?
   d. Where does it happen?
   e. When does it happen?

2. What is your goal (what do you want your dog to do instead of behaving aggressively)?
3. How will you get there (what techniques will you use to help him learn safe, friendly alternatives to aggression)?
4. How will you maintain the change?
   a. What do we need to pay attention to after the training is done to ensure that the aggression doesn't return?

In earlier chapters, you learned to observe your dog's behavior and figure out the situations under which it occurred. Then you elaborated on this and began to make notes of the dog's behavior chain leading up to aggression, the situation(s) in which the aggression occurred, who was around, and when it happened. Continue to take notes daily. This log will be very helpful to you in identifying behaviors and situations, so if you see something, write it down.

There are probably things you can do to improve your dog's behavior without using CAT, some of which will be quite important. For example, maybe your dog behaves worse in the evening or when he first wakes up. And maybe he behaves better just after breakfast. If your dog behaves badly later in the day and when he first wakes up, but he acts better after he eats, what's the most obvious thing to zero in on? If you only feed him once a day, maybe adding a second meal later in the day could make him more comfortable so that he doesn't get irritable in the evening. Feeding him earlier in the morning might keep him from being so hard to handle when he wakes up. If you're concerned about him gaining weight if he gets an extra meal, consider dividing his meals into two portions and serve one in the morning and one in the evening. We

started to do this at the shelter where I worked years ago, and the dogs became easier to handle without increasing the amount of money we spent on food or risking making them overweight. Twenty-four hours is a long time to wait for a meal, and most of us get cranky if we're hungry. There are a number of small adjustments you can identify by keeping records on a regular basis.

As you decide where to conduct your first CAT sessions, think about what situations would be the most valuable to you. Remember, your training scenario will be a fake version of the real situations your dog has problems in. If you want to be able to walk your dog past other people on walks in your neighborhood, that's the type of scenario you want to start with, using cooperative helpers.

Look at the situation you've chosen and think about the practicalities of setting it up. Often it's helpful and necessary

to break the training plan down a little to make it more feasible. Let's say your dog is aggressive toward other people on the sidewalk, but mostly after dinner, when there are dozens of people and dogs out taking walks. You'll want to do your training sessions in the same place but start working at a less busy time of day to make it less overwhelming for your dog. If your neighborhood is always crowded, you may have no choice but to start working in a quieter neighborhood at first. This is not ideal because you want your dog to be nice in your neighborhood, but your dog can't learn if there is too much stress in the environment.

Following, I will detail the CAT procedure to rehabilitate a dog who is aggressive toward other people and dogs when out on walks. I use the terms *helper* for the human helper, *helper dog* for the helper dog, and *rehab dog* for the aggressive dog being rehabilitated.

PREPARATION

1. Decide what training gear you will use and/or how you will safely arrange the environment. If the rehab dog will be wearing a muzzle, you should have muzzle-trained him in advance.

2. Identify the person who is most often handling the dog or near the dog when he behaves aggressively. If no one is usually nearby, a camera and someone to carefully watch the action on the camera can be substituted.

3. Without the rehab dog present, mark the boundaries that will indicate how

Ready for training!

Use two hands to hold the leash.

far the dog can move. For example, if you're going to hold the dog's leash, the boundary will be the distance from your body to the dog's head when the leash is fully extended and held securely. Always hold the leash in two hands. One hand should hold the loop of the handle, and the other should hold the length of the leash. You should give the leash some slack unless the dog is pulling it tight. The handler should be ready to prevent the dog from reaching the helper with any part of the dog's body.

4. The helper should wear protective gear appropriate to the dog's aggression. If the dog has ever bitten, especially if it was a bad bite, the helper should wear protective gloves and long pants, preferably sturdy jeans, and boots.

5. If there will be a helper dog, make sure that the helper dog's handler has a pouch full of desirable treats at all times.

6. Have separate water bowls available to the rehab dog and the helper dog.

THE PROCEDURE

1. The helper and helper dog will begin at a distance sufficiently far from the rehab dog that the dog notices the helper but does not react aggressively. This determines what dog trainers call the *threshold*. If you're farther away than this threshold, you're considered below threshold. *Below threshold* is good. If you move closer than the threshold, and the dog reacts aggressively, you're *over threshold*. Avoid going over threshold.

2. The helper marks the starting point. Then the helper and helper dog walk toward the rehab dog about two small steps. Notice or mark the new location. If the rehab dog does not react aggressively, this new location will be the starting point, or threshold, for the next approach.

a. If the rehab dog behaves aggressively, look carefully for any behavior besides aggression and walk away. If the dog's eruption is severe, start the next approach from a farther distance and stop farther away than was done on this attempt.

Avoid pushing the rehab dog over threshold.

i. If the rehab dog does not behave aggressively and instead offers any appropriate behavior (other than just shutting down), the helper turns away quickly and walks away from the rehab dog. Some dogs erupt in a huge way, and the helper must be ready to turn around and walk away the instant that the rehab dog offers a desirable alternative behavior, even if it doesn't last very long.

ii. Note: The rehab dog's handler should not cue the rehab dog on what to do. He or she should let the dog figure it out on his own. If the handler is doing the thinking and deciding, the dog won't be the one doing the learning. Let the dog have choices within safe parameters so that he can learn that his safe choices are very effective.

b. The helper should pet the helper dog, provide treats or otherwise make the dog comfortable.

c. The helper will wait between ten and thirty seconds before walking forward again. The specific amount of time isn't critical, just long enough that it is worthwhile for the helper dog. The helper should not immediately walk right back to the rehab dog. Change up the amount of time between approaches so it doesn't become predictable for the rehab dog.

d. On the next approach, the helper and helper dog will come just a short distance closer to the rehab dog, with the goal of not getting close enough to make the dog behave aggressively. Usually these increments will be quite small. For some dogs, they need to be teeny-tiny. You can vary the increments each time to see what works, but the helper should not take giant steps closer.

   i. Sometimes dogs will not erupt until the helper turns to walk away. If this happens, the helper should stop, wait for the dog to offer a more desirable behavior, and then walk away again. You may need to repeat this several times before the rehab dog offers a good enough response to walk away.

  ii. The rehab dog should be allowed to see the helper walking away. This is his reward. We want him to feel the relief that comes with seeing something he doesn't like move farther away. I call this the "whew!" effect. We also want him to see that his old aggressive responses no longer work to chase the scary person or dog away; now, only friendly and safe behaviors work.

 iii. The helper person should change his or her body language during each approach to help the rehab dog learn that the new rules don't apply only when the helper is acting cautious, or perky, or commanding. The new rules need to be applied to all kinds of behavior. Have the helper turn to the left after one approach and turn to the right on another. If these changes create enough difference for the rehab dog, you may need to repeat the approach at the same distance from the rehab dog multiple times before coming any closer.

e. The helper and helper dog will now repeat Step 2 until they are within a few feet of the rehab dog but still at a safe distance.

f. The helper will approach to the new threshold several times while watching the rehab dog for signs of curious behavior. The dog may tilt his head, sniff toward the helper, or try to move forward in a friendly way without lunging or behaving aggressively in any other way.

g. If the rehab dog continually acts curious, move on to Step 3. If he stiffens or behaves aggressively, back up in your training and work through the same steps again, starting at a place where the dog was behaving well. Come closer to the dog in smaller steps this time to make it easier for him.

3. Once the helper and helper dog can approach the rehab dog's boundaries safely multiple times, the helper and the rehab dog's handler will go for a parallel walk with the dogs. A parallel walk is a side-by-side walk in neutral

territory. The dogs should be far enough away from each other that they can't reach each other, but they should be close enough to be aware of each other's presence. As the walk continues, the helper should move farther away and then closer, to a safe distance, repeatedly. If the rehab dog behaves well, the helper moves slightly farther away while continuing the walk. If the rehab dog behaves aggressively, everyone should stop and wait for a more desirable response before continuing to walk casually along.

4. After a long period of time, when the rehab dog has consistently offered friendly and safe behaviors, allow the rehab dog to approach the helper and helper dog from a safe distance as long as his behavior stays friendly and loose and as long as the helper dog is comfortable with it. If the rehab dog is stiff, either keep walking or do a little more of the approach-and-retreat type of work.

You can work these steps in long sessions with lots of comfort and rest breaks, or you can do shorter sessions (which often work best with people's schedules) and just start over again the next time. As I've written before, each time you start over, you're likely to lose a little bit of ground. Just keep working and, if possible, keep the sessions, whether long or short, close together.

SHAPING FRIENDLY BEHAVIOR

As you work through these steps, your dog will not always offer the exact behavior you want, so it can be tricky to figure out when the helper should turn and walk away. You're going to have to take this in bite-sized pieces. The first time you approach the dog, you might find that he just barks and barks and barks and goes on and on and on. Wait for him to take a breath between barks, which will make the break between barks a little longer than the rest. That's when the helper walks away.

At first, you'll take what you can get, even if it's not much. If you're not getting a lot to work with, reward a smaller change. Consider having the helper move farther away from the rehab dog and starting over from there. Or have the helper turn in a different direction to face away from the rehab dog. Over time, the helper will need to change positions with respect to the rehab dog, but while you're building behavior, the important thing to do is "get the behavior," as Bob Bailey says. You've got to get the behavior you want before you can strengthen it.

Later, you'll stop reinforcing these barely desirable behaviors and wait just a little longer to see what else the dog will offer. After you've been working for a while, he will offer other behaviors that you'll need to "grab" by walking away as soon as he does them. If he turns his head, if he turns his body, if he lifts a paw or even just an eyebrow, walk away immediately. Or maybe the tone of his bark begins to change. Sometime a dog will start out sounding very fierce, but, over time, as that behavior doesn't work, his voice will sound different, as if he's trying something new to see if it will work.

Importantly, if the dog just isn't offering better behaviors, the goal is to make it easier, not harder, for him to succeed. Maybe try a different helper dog. Maybe walk away when he blinks instead of waiting for him to turn his head.

Remember that the more you reinforce stillness, the harder the work will get. Just because a dog is still doesn't mean that he is calm. Often, a dog will figure out that you always walk away when he doesn't do much. Try to walk away when the dog is moving. If the dog doesn't move, get the helper to walk him around the work area a bit and walk away when he looks at you.

TAKING IT ON THE ROAD—GENERALIZATION

There are some key elements to remember while doing this work. One is, obviously, that you will adjust the procedure based on where your dog's aggression occurs. If your dog barks at your spouse when he or she approaches the couch, the spouse will be the helper and will walk away and return until he or she can approach and sit on the couch safely. Sometimes there will be some "false sits" before your helper-spouse can sit down.

There are some times when you'll encounter unexpected people or dogs on your walks in the neighborhood. If an off-leash dog approaches your dog, sometimes you just have to cut your losses to avoid a fight. A can of citronella spray (which is not normally my favorite way to deal with dog problems) may be just what the situation calls for in an emergency. If the other dog is not under control, you will need to be prepared. If a person walks up to you and your dog, you have to be assertive and say, "Do not touch my dog. He is in training." The person may not like it, but he or she won't get bitten, and your dog won't go to quarantine for biting.

Always have your dog wear his muzzle while out on walks whether or not you are in training. Muzzles have a way of deterring most people, even if the dog is not aggressive at all. If asked why your dog wears a muzzle, just say, "Just in case!" That's all they need to know.

There are far too many situations to explain in this one book, unfortunately,

Generalization takes your training into the real world.

but here's what you need to focus on: What does my dog want right now? What is he doing to get it? How can I change his current behavior (aggression) to friendly behavior? And how can I make it easy for him to do the right thing?

It's also important to understand that one successful training session does not equal a rehabilitated dog unless there is only one narrow situation in which aggression occurs. Most dogs need a process called *generalization*, which basically means that the training must occur in a variety of situations, with a variety of people or dogs, in different locations, with different people around (even if the person in the setup is not someone toward whom the dog behaves aggressively), doing different things.

Even if you're looking at something as simple as teaching a sit, the dog needs to understand that "Sit" means the same thing when he's alone with you in the kitchen, when Grandma is here, when Matthew has just arrived home from school, and when the FedEx truck has just pulled up outside. The dog should always get something he likes in each of these situations. As Bob Bailey said in an interview with the *Fort Worth Star Telegram* years ago, "Give them something they like in exchange for playing your silly games." Sometimes a treat is just the thing the dog will work for. If you need him to learn something new, like sitting when there's lawnmower noise outside, a treat just might do the trick.

SUPERVISED PLAY

If you have a dog who behaves aggressively to other dogs, your dog is not pining for a canine friend. Many times, owners come to our shelters looking for a friend for their reactive dog because he surely must be lonely and need a friend. No. His aggression toward other dogs is his way of saying to you, "I don't like other dogs, and I don't want to be near them." He needs *you*. He does not need other dogs. Don't take this dog to a dog park. Doing the CAT treatment with your dog may help him be able to play with other dogs, but there is still a chance that he could revert to old behaviors.

A better option for after you've successfully completed CAT training is to set up controlled play dates with dogs and owners you know in environments where both dogs can be given a break before they get overwhelmed. A dog who gets along well with other dogs has some hallmarks of appropriate play that you should look for, one of which is that he plays for a while and then takes a break. During the break, neither dog keeps hassling the other dog to play. They may run and tumble for five minutes and then stand or lie down, looking off into the distance, at the same time. That's desirable dog behavior.

If one of the dogs doesn't let the other dog take a break, the pushier dog should be led away on leash to do a little treat training or to rest in his crate. Sometimes dogs are like rowdy two-year-olds who don't know they're exhausted, and they benefit from a little help settling down. If the dog who wants a break is your aggressive dog, giving him a break before he does anything bad can be the difference between his remembering his CAT lessons and his deciding that he better go back to his old ways because the other dog isn't acting right. If your aggressive dog won't give the other dog a break, he is probably overly excited, and you may be heading for a problem if you don't calmly intervene.

The same thing will apply to behaving in safe, friendly ways instead of with aggression. If your dog has learned that behaving nicely to people in the house instead of charging them with bared teeth pays off with people not hurting him, he needs to learn that this also applies in the backyard, in the parking lot you cross through on your walks, and in the car. You'll have to practice in all of these situations (or, more accurately, in the situations that are important to you and your dog) for your dog to be successful.

The way generalization usually works is that after trying out several new situations, a lightbulb goes off in the dog's head, and he realizes that this is how the world now works everywhere. But how many times it will take depends on many factors. How long has the dog been behaving aggressively? How many times has he been rewarded for aggression in the past because he was able to chase away things he didn't like? In how many unique situations has he been aggressive? How often has aggression continued to work since you introduced the CAT training protocol? (This is where your management tools are essential. You must prevent the dog from being rewarded for aggressive behavior, if at all possible. I am not saying that your dog should be left defenseless when he's in danger; what I mean is that your dog should not be thrust into situations that he thinks he needs to control with his ferocity.)

You have to be your dog's guardian and ensure that he isn't immersed in situations he cannot control without using his teeth. You wouldn't take your dog to a dog fight, right? Don't put him into other situations that overwhelm him, either. You already know what situations overwhelm your dog. Watch out to avoid them in the future. Keep interactions short. End interactions on a positive note. Avoid interactions that your dog is uncomfortable in. Instruct other people on how to behave around your dog and keep him away from people who might not cooperate. Avoid places where there may be a lot of people or dogs who might overwhelm him.

THE SWITCHOVER EFFECT

There's a question that comes up again and again: Will my dog always have to be rewarded with having other people or dogs go away? I want him to like other people and dogs. I don't want him to always hate

them. Yes, no, and maybe are all correct answers.

When you've successfully completed the CAT procedure through generalization in all situations in which your dog is likely to react with aggression, and when you've conducted the procedure thoroughly, you will start to see something we termed *the switchover effect*. What happens with animals who have been trained with increased distance from people or animals they find aversive is a bit of a surprise: the animals often change their minds about these "threats." When I first meet a dog with severe aggression, he may look like tearing my head off would make him incredibly satisfied. But when I finish all the steps that we went through earlier, the ferocious dog begins to solicit my attention in friendly ways.

The switchover is the most dangerous point of the CAT procedure, and underestimating the risk is a bad idea.

It can be very tricky to tell if the dog is actually ready for an interaction; this is why I advise parallel walking once we can approach the dog closely rather than jumping right into personal contact with a helper until there is absolutely no question that the dog will behave in a friendly way. Even when you think switchover could happen, there is still risk. We want as many opportunities as possible to evaluate the dog's behavior. We want to see if he continues to hold his body tightly or if he loosens up and his muscles relax. Look at your observation notes from the earlier chapters and understand when your dog acts most friendly and when he acts least friendly, and what is happening at those times. He may be at his most friendly when he's alone with you. What does that look like? How is it different from what he does in the moments before he chases or bites

someone? Apply that information to the observations at the end of the approach-and-retreat part of the training.

After that, if the rehab dog wants to sniff, and the helper person or helper dog is OK with it, let him sniff. I recommend that you keep the initial contact brief and that the handler hold the leash securely and the helper move away before trying again. Check the rehab dog's behavior and see if he's still looking chill and interested. If he is, try it again. I've had many dogs come forward and lick my hand and nestle close to me after going through this process, but I still walk away many times more. As Dr. Rosales told me, "This is how we got the good behavior. We don't want to stop it now."

But the switchover interactions, when they happen, are beautiful to behold. As one owner said when her dog took that giant leap, "Lennie! You have a friend!"

Leashes pulled tightly can increase the dogs' anxiety.

12
CONCLUSION

This book has provided you with some lessons, some safety measures, and a procedure that has been proven to work by many pet owners and trainers around the world. Most of the people who did the work were trainers, but many pet owners who needed help with their dogs' aggressive behavior have worked with it, too. You are already the one handing your aggressive dog. You deserve to know how to help him look at the world in a new way that will make your life, and his, better. You want him and everyone in your world to be safe, so it's a matter of deciding if you can accomplish the CAT procedure with the physical skills, stamina, resources, and tools that you now have.

There are other ways you can work with aggression, and some of them will help you immensely, especially in managing your dog's aggression and helping him realize that good things happen when he is good. Nevertheless, I encourage you to think about using the outcome your dog has already shown that he will work for and to reinforce behaviors you know will be safer for your dog, your family, your friends, yourself, and your community. Your dog isn't looking for treats when he aggresses toward people or dogs. He is trying to make them go away. Let's show him that people will not bother him if he's nice. You will accomplish this by orchestrating his world so that it is a safer place by only exposing him to people and animals he is ready to be around. When you start taking him into the situations you've been working on using CAT, you'll keep those interactions quite short and do everything you can to end on a high note. Walk away while things are going well, just like your helpers walked away when your dog was being good in the CAT procedure.

Your dog sees someone in the distance, and he's concerned. He looks around for an exit, but then he remembers that he's on his leash and won't be able to get away. In the past, he always froze, stared, lowered his head, growled, backed up, lunged, and tried to bite. Now, as soon as you see him looking for an exit, you give him one. You walk with him in a different direction that won't require him to interact with the worrisome stranger. This is one part of the solution. You will now be aware and respectful of what your dog needs in order to behave well.

Your dog sees someone approaching and freezes. But instead of the stranger walking away, this time you've carefully arranged for someone you know to turn and walk away the second he moves his head or paw. He gets to practice lots of alternatives to aggression. He gets to try things that are easier and work just as well, even better. And he starts to choose these better behaviors even when you're out on regular walks in your neighborhood. He does these good behaviors first and puts aggression behind him.

Your job is to proactively set up your dog's world to ensure that his friendly behaviors continue to pay off better than anything else he could possibly do. Although you will always need to be your dog's advocate, your life will be easier with CAT procedures in your tool kit. Your family and friends will be safer, and your dog will get a new outlook on life that will help him feel better in the world.

INDEX

PHOTO CREDITS

ABOUT THE AUTHOR

Kellie Snider, MS, has BS and MS degrees in behavior analysis from the University of North Texas. Her graduate thesis, *A Constructional Canine Aggression Treatment*, was conducted under the direction of Dr. Jesús Rosales-Ruiz and resulted in several years of traveling across the United States, Canada, and England to present the rehabilitation procedure for aggressive dogs to trainers and behaviorists in seminar settings. Kellie has presented topics on a variety of animal behavior-related subjects in university symposia, colloquia, seminars, webinars, radio programs, and conferences.

In 2007, Kellie won awards for humane dog–dog aggression rehabilitation and humane dog–human aggression rehabilitation from the International Positive Dog Training Association. Kellie's work in shelter behavior has presented ongoing opportunities to observe and provide behavior modification for shelter dogs and cats with a variety of behavior challenges. She was hired by the SPCA of Texas in 2008 to develop an animal-behavior program and remained there for nearly ten years. She then took the position of Shelter Manager III with Dallas Animal Services, where she oversees all aspects of animal intake and outcomes for the city of Dallas. From 2012 to 2016, she served as the behavior consultant for PetSmart Charities Rescue Waggin' dog-transport program, for which she designed a behavior assessment and trained employees at fifty-six shelters in transporting animals to other shelters, where they were more likely to be adopted, thus helping reduce euthanasia of shelter animals across the country. She is a task force member of Fear Free Pets (www.fearfreepets.com) and a licensed Family Paws Pets Educator. She is also vice president of the National Association of Animal Behaviorists.

Kellie lives in the Dallas, Texas area. She is married and has two adult sons, three cats, and two dogs. When not working with animals, she creates art (watercolor, colored pencil, and wool hooked rugs) and writes.

PRAISE FROM KELLIE'S COLLEAGUES AND CLIENTS

"Kellie Snider is a fierce advocate for dogs and those who love them, especially the furry souls lashing out with fear—or hiding in whimpering retreat from the world. Her innovative science-based and humane CAT approach...will save dogs and pet-people relationships. This book is world-changing for dog lovers!"

—Amy Shojai, CABC, animal behavior consultant, and author

"It's very easy to get caught up in the emotions of dealing with a dog that is reactive to people or other dogs, but Kellie Snider uses science to move past the emotional states and digs into the core of classical and operant conditioning when working with dogs to help them past their reactions. This is a must-read for anyone working on behaviors that fall into the spectrum of aggression and will give trainers and behavior experts the foundation for helping more dogs move into an increased and relaxed state of mind."

—Nan Arthur, CDBC, CPDT-KSA, KPACTP, Karen Pryer Dog Training Academy faculty, certification instructor for dog*tec Dog Walking Academy, certified DogSafe First Aid instructor, and author of *Chill Out Fido! How to Calm your Dog*

"So, my human mom brought this new dog into *my* house, and I was fine with him until he turned a year old. I tried to tell her, 'He's not a puppy anymore, so he needs to go.' But she insisted he stay. I tried to get more insistent...but mom was getting increasingly frustrated at my escalations. Then somebody gave her some advice—she said it was just a simple thing, but it totally changed my perspective. It reminded me how much I really do like this little brother, and now we are pals again. Mom keeps saying, 'Thank you, Kellie!' I guess I agree with her."

—Caleb, the Cairn Terrier

"Kellie gave me one seemingly innocuous piece of advice to help my two fighting Cairns get past their issues. That piece of advice completely changed the dynamics in our home, and our two warring Cairns are now happily 'brothers' again! We owe the peace in our home to her. Thank you, Kellie!"

—Tina Vial

"As one of the nation's top animal behaviorists, Kellie Snider has dedicated her life to transforming scared or misunderstood shelter animals into happy, healthy family pets. She never shies away from tough topics and strives every day in every way to bring out the best in dogs who deserve loving homes. Got dog? You need to get this book."

—Arden Moore, The Pet Health and Safety Coach and author of *Fit Dog*

"When I began my dog-training journey, Kellie Snider was one of the first people I found who was willing to share her knowledge of behavior analysis in everyday training of pets. She inspired me to continue my own education, and I continue to learn from her research and work with shelter dogs."

—Barb Gadola, CPDT-KA, Distinctive Dog Training LLC

"Kellie Snider is one of those amazing trainers I would trust to handle my own dogs. This incredible protocol has saved countless dogs already, and now it can save countless more."

—Melissa Alexander, author of *Click for Joy: Questions and Answers from Clicker Trainers and Their Dogs*

"I first met Kellie in 2008 at a CAT seminar, and I was fascinated by her outside-the-box approach to teaching better social behavior to dogs with aggression issues. Over the years, Kellie's been a generous source of guidance to me and countless others who have made dog behavior their lives. I've been successful borrowing concepts from Kellie's work to help scores of dogs with a variety of issues. A thorough understanding of CAT is an invaluable addition to any dog trainer's toolbox."

—Barbara Davis, CPDT-KA, CDBC

"Kellie Snider has worked extensively with fearful and aggressive dogs and has honed her techniques to be maximally effective. Beyond her years of practical experience, she completed her master's thesis on effectively using CAT and has the knowledge of behavioral principles that our field needs. Her knowledge of applied animal behavior and her experience make her a much-needed resource, and I look forward to her sharing her knowledge with other practitioners."

—Erica Feuerbacher, PhD, BCBA-D, CPDT-KA